If I Were a Man,
I'd Marry
Me

If I Were a Man, I'd Marry Me

P. S. WALL

Ballantine Books • New York

A Ballantine Book
Published by The Ballantine Publishing Group

Copyright © 1999 by P. S. Wall

All rights reserved under International
and Pan-American Copyright Conventions. Published
in the United States by The Ballantine Publishing Group, a division
of Random House, Inc., New York, and simultaneously in
Canada by Random House of Canada Limited, Toronto.
The contents of this work were originally published in the
author's syndicated column, "Off the Wall."

Ballantine and colophon are registered trademarks of Random House, Inc.

www.randomhouse.com/BB/

LIBRARY OF CONGRESS CATALOGING-IN-PUBLICATION DATA
Wall, P.S. (Paula S.), 1954–
If I were a man, I'd marry me / P.S. Wall.
p.   cm.
ISBN 0-345-43032-8 (alk. paper)
I. Title.
PN4874.W278A3   1999
814'.54—dc21   99-13478

Text design by Holly Johnson

Manufactured in the United States of America

First Edition: August 1999

10   9   8   7   6   5   4   3   2   1

For Sheila, Cortney, Larry, Brenda, Cuz, and Cindy.
I get by with a little help from my friends.

Contents

Jockey Strap Love . . .

With Friends Like These, Who Needs Drugs?

The Nut Doesn't Fall Far from the Family Tree

If I Were a Man, I'd Marry Me

Jockey Strap Love . . .

Jockey Strap Love

My girlfriend is dating a younger man. Let me clarify that. Actually, she's dating an embryo. I have jeans older than this boy.

This afternoon we met for lunch, and I can't say it went that well. Through the whole meal I couldn't decide whether to rip his shirt off or cut his chicken into bite-size pieces.

I will admit, sitting there next to her baby beau, Kat looks great. It's as though she's found the fountain of youth. Or at least a twenty-ounce returnable bottle.

"Isn't she *bold?*" the kid says as he watches Kat walk across the restaurant to the ladies' room.

I look up from my penne pasta to see who in the world he's talking about. Kat's a good friend and I love her like a sister, but I can't say *bold* is an adjective that immediately comes to mind. *Italic*, maybe, but not *bold.*

"See, the thing about older women is," he says, "they are just *so-ooo* together. I mean, like, they know what they want and they go for it."

Suddenly a choir of angels bursts into the Hallelujah Chorus and tears well up in my eyes. I have been blessed with a vision. I'm not getting older. I'm getting more together.

"And . . ." the kid adds, his mouth full, "they pick up the check."

Why a woman would date a younger guy is a mystery to

me. Intellectually, I realize age doesn't have anything to do with anything. I know fifty-year-old women who have twenty-year-old bodies, and forty-year-old women who are dumb as squash.

But let's face it, boys do not drop out of the womb gracious creatures. If you fall in love with a younger guy, it's like trying to have a relationship with a jock strap. There's just no give, and expansion is totally out of the question.

So I ask my cousin to explain it to me. She's a psychologist. She knows about these things.

"Either it's a classic case of a woman's pathetic attempt to regain the lost exhilaration of youth," Cuz says analytically. "Or she's got the hots for young studs."

Guys are like dogs. You wish you could take them all home when they're puppies. But after they've howled all night and slobbered all over everything, you come to realize that the ones who are already trained are much easier to live with.

I will admit there is something about a young guy that causes the heart to flutter. But for me, it is mostly those rare moments when the man he might become manages to flicker through.

It takes time and experience for a boy to ripen into a man of quiet character. I'll take sophistication and wisdom over youth any day of the week. Give me the man who knows what he wants and goes for it.

And of course, one who can pick up the check.

The Mattress Authority

Flying back from the East Coast, I got seated next to a hooker.

"Actually, I prefer escort," she says.

"Sorry," I say.

"No offense taken." She shrugs as she checks her lip liner in a fourteen-karat-gold compact.

They overbooked the flight, and Sweetie insisted I use the upgrade ticket to first class. I'm not sure what he wants, but you can bet I'll end up paying for it—one way or another.

Stretching up from my seat, I scan the plane. As far back as I can see, people are packed in like cigarettes. I finally spot Sweetie seated in front of the lavatory. Pinched between two albino sumo wrestlers, he looks like a rectal thermometer. As the flight attendant pulls the curtain closed between us, I wave. I'm sure he would have waved back if he could have pulled his arms free.

If someone tries to tell you there isn't a difference between first class and coach, stick a pin in their behind. If they jump, you'll know they're lying.

"Man, my bed doesn't feel this good," I say, oozing into the plush leather seat.

"A mattress is the most important purchase a person makes," the hooker says as she slowly rubs hand lotion on each manicured finger.

"Really?"

"Neck problems, headaches, stress—improper back support."

"No kidding?"

"Absolutely." She nods. "You get what you pay for."

I have no doubt this woman knows whereof she speaks. She has *mattress authority* written all over her.

"Take shoes," she continues. Stretching her silk-stockinged leg out into the aisle, she shows me her stiletto. This is not a shoe. It's a size 7$\frac{1}{2}$ Maserati.

"You want to try them on?" she asks as she spritzes behind each ear with Chanel.

Kicking off my Timberlands, I slip into what can only be described as chocolate for your feet. "Oh," I moan, eyes rolling back. "Oooooh, yes!"

"I have them custom-made in Italy," she says. "Fifteen hundred dollars a pair."

"Worth every penny," I sigh. When it comes to comfortable shoes, I'm easily corrupted.

While they're ladling out the gruel back in bourgeoisie, our flight attendant shows up with a tray of champagne. Shaking her head, the escort waves it away.

"I never drink when I'm working," she says, sipping bottled water.

"You're working?" I ask, looking around. "Like . . . right now?"

The escort nods to a huddle of businessmen in front of us. I immediately zero in on a dark-haired guy who with the right light and a good imagination could pass for Richard Gere.

"WHOA!" I growl.

"Not him," she says, tilting her nod. "*Him*."

"Whoa." I frown.

This poor guy would have to pay a mosquito to bite him.

The escort has just launched into her philosophy on waxing versus shaving when the pilot tells us we're landing. Time sure flies when you're living above your means.

"Well," I say as I pull my knapsack from the overhead, "I really enjoyed it."

"If you ever get to Miami . . ." the escort says, handing me her embossed business card.

"If you ever get to Nashville . . ." I say, scratching my name and number on the back of a cocktail napkin.

"Oh, by the way," I add, thinking what are the odds of my ever having this opportunity again, "in your professional opinion, which guys are . . . well, the best?"

Glancing over at her "date," the escort motions for me to lean close. "The ones who don't have to pay for it," she whispers.

About this time, Sweetie hobbles through the curtain out of cattle class, dragging his left side like Quasimodo.

"Oh, they all pay for it," I say as I drape Sweetie's limp arm over my shoulder. "But for most of us, it's more of a barter system."

Blue-Bellied Lizards

If there were a Human Services Department for pets, they'd probably deem me unfit, and Cat would be placed in a foster cathouse.

"How did it happen?" the vet asks as he studies Cat's eye. Dr. Don is wearing black magnifying goggles. His eyes are two inches across and he looks like a wall-eyed pike.

"He got in a fight with a blue jay," I say.

Eyebrows raised, Dr. Don rolls his magnified eyes to his intern.

"You let Cat go outside?" she gasps.

We live in the country, for pete's sake. It's not like he hangs out at crack houses with the boys in the hood.

"You poor, poor baby," the intern coos into Cat's ear, glaring at me.

The fur ball, of course, is eating this up. Leaning his moth-eaten head against her lab coat, he looks up at her with his good eye and purrs pathetically.

"His cornea is torn," Dr. Don says as he puts a little patch over Cat's eye. "It'll take a while to heal. Under NO CIRCUMSTANCES is he to go outside."

The intern hands me a bag of medicine that costs three times more than I paid for the fleabag cat, and a brochure on CAT PARENTING.

"I'll need to see him in a week," Dr. Don says as he studies his cuticles through his goggles.

Donning my Ray-Bans, I slink through the waiting room.

"I have never been so humiliated in my life!" I say as I snap the seat belt around Cat's carrier. "Having to peel you off the intern was an especially nice touch!"

Sensing we are not alone, I look up. The man sitting in the car next to us is watching me like I'm the Sports Channel.

"I'm talking to a cat!" I yell at his window. "You got a problem with that?"

"Women are crazy," he mutters to the Doberman sitting in the seat next to him.

When we get home, I sit Cat down on the couch for a serious chewing out.

"You're grounded!" I say, shaking my finger in his furry little face. "The next time you see grass, it'll be growing on top of your kitty-cat coffin!"

It takes Cat exactly fourteen minutes to break out through the dryer vent. And when he finally shows up, he has a six-inch lizard clamped to his ear like a pierced earring.

"He looks like Captain Hook," Sweetie says as we stare at our stubby-tailed, one-eyed Manx, with a blue-bellied lizard dangling from his ear.

I weigh my options. I can admit Cat was outside, or I can tell Dr. Don we have six-inch snapping lizards running rampant in our living room.

"There's no way we're going to the vet," I say. "Pull him off."

"*You* pull him off!" Sweetie says, backing up. "I'm not touching that thing!"

Pulling on a leather ski glove, I give the lizard a tug and his tail falls off.

Next we try cold. While I hold Cat, Sweetie packs the lizard in crushed ice. The lizard doesn't blink, but Cat turns blue and I'm pretty sure the tip of his ear has frostbite.

"All animals are afraid of fire," Sweetie assures me as he flicks a Bic and waves it in front of the lizard.

Ssssst and Cat's whiskers are history. Meanwhile, the lizard is roasting marshmallows.

"We're going to have to cut his head off," Sweetie says, pulling out the wire cutters.

Cat's good eye swells to the size of a saucer.

"Not you, stupid," Sweetie mutters to Cat.

Sweetie clamps down on the lizard's neck, and just as he's about to snip, the lizard drops off—taking a chunk of Cat's ear with him—and scurries under the couch.

While Sweetie and I watch, our stubby-tailed, one-eyed, one-eared, whiskerless cat calmly licks the memory of his manhood.

"What do you say we keep the lizard," Sweetie says, "and throw away the cat."

Through the Wringer

Leaning over the laundry basket, Sweetie slowly picks up the knotted wad of faded wool. Looking up at me in horror, he stares at me like I'm a serial sweater murderer.

"What have you done to it?" he gasps, the ball of wool that was once his favorite sweater shredding in his fingers.

A girl can be skilled at only so many domestic things. I cook. I clean. I've read the *Kama Sutra*. So I can't wash a load of clothes. Tie my tubes and call the sheriff.

"It's just a sweater," I say. "Get over it."

"Mother gave me this sweater." Sweetie chokes as he cups the lifeless little carcass of cashmere in his palm.

"Then Mama should have washed it," I mumble.

"Cold," Sweetie says. "Very cold."

I assume he's referring to the water temperature I should have used.

I trace my war with the wash back to my grandmother's Maytag wringer washer. Parked on the back porch between the chopping block and the pickle crock, it stuck out like an alien robot.

Every Saturday morning, foaming, sloshing, and wringer whirring, the tub would moonwalk across the porch like it was preparing for takeoff. Finger in my face, Grandma would threaten me if I so much as looked at the thing. Of course, as soon as the screen door slammed, I was climbing all over it.

13

Having permanently pressed every bug in the vicinity, I was branching out into vegetables, and was in the process of squashing a crookneck squash when the thing grabbed me. As it ate its way down my arm, I weighed my options. I could face Grandma's wrath or spend the rest of my life looking like a peekapoo.

Grandma found me screaming, the Maytag dragging me, kicking and half-eaten, down the porch. My arm plumped back to normal after a couple of days, but the burning Grandma gave my behind remains to this day.

Hence, from that day forth, left alone with a washer and dryer, I am a terrorist. I can fade the colorfast, put wrinkles in the wrinkle-free, and shrink the unshrinkable. My solution to matching socks—don't wear any.

For Sweetie, on the other hand, laundry is a science. His whites are white, his colors bright. The boy actually takes the clothes out of the dryer the same day he puts them in.

You could bale the grass in the front yard and take a shower under the roof during a hard rain, but you can bet Sweetie's underwear will always be as white as the driven snow.

The solution to our laundry differences seems obvious to me. "Knock yourself out," I say, feet kicked up and cruising the reruns.

"What if I run off with Michelle Pfeiffer?" Sweetie asks. "Who'll presoak your stains?"

"Sweetie," I say, popping the top on a Dr Pepper, "I'm willing to take that chance."

Apparently, Sweetie isn't. Standing in front of the washer like a professor explaining quantum physics, Sweetie proceeds to lecture me.

"The secret to the perfect wash is separation," Sweetie says as he divides the clothes into perfectly color-coded piles.

"Now," he says, holding up a white sock, "where do I put it?"

I give him a look that tells him exactly where I'd like to see it go.

"By dissolving the detergent prior to putting the separated clothes into the washer," Sweetie says, holding the measuring cup up to the light, "you will achieve a more thorough cleansing."

It occurs to me there is something very sweet about watching Sweetie meticulously do laundry as if he's preparing to split the atom.

"Did your grandmother teach you how to wash clothes?" I ask as I wad up a clean towel and free-throw it into the hamper.

"Nah," Sweetie says, holding a clean pair of jeans with his chin. "Granny didn't believe a man should do laundry. A girl I dated in college taught me everything I know."

Smoothing the crease like a straight edge, Sweetie sighs nostalgically. "Boy, could that woman tumble and dry."

Harley

"Just because you can afford a Harley-Davidson motorcycle," the salesman says, "doesn't necessarily mean you deserve to own one."

"I hear what you're sayin', man," Sweetie says, doing his best James Dean.

"Had a lawyer try one on this morning," the salesman says as he picks bug parts out of his teeth with a knife. "Like putting a tutu on a hog."

The salesman spits, and insect wings splatter the linoleum. "No way I could sell it to him."

"Hey," Sweetie shrugs sympathetically, "either you have it or you don't."

Arms crossed and eyes narrowed, the salesman inspects Sweetie up and down. "So," he says, "you think you're ready to ride the wild boar?"

Handing me his briefcase, Sweetie neatly folds his suit coat and drapes it over my arm.

"Scratch the chrome," Fly says, eyeing Sweetie's cuff links, "and I'll have to hurt you."

"Sorry," Sweetie mutters.

Jerking his twenty-four-karat *Wall Street Week* cuff links off, Sweetie drops them into my purse. Then, grabbing the handle, Sweetie swings a Rockport, with orthotic arch support, over the seat and melts into the saddle.

"Oh, Mama!" Sweetie moans.

It has always been Sweetie's dream to ride to California on a Harley. While a Harley may have played a major part in a dream or two of mine, you can bet it was parked.

"Hop on," Fly says to me, nodding with his ponytail.

While the driver's seat on a Harley is like a La-Z-Boy recliner, the passenger's seat was obviously designed by the Marquis de Sade. It's six inches higher than the driver's, and approximately the size of a hot dog bun. I pucker just looking at it.

"So, let me get this straight," I say. "You expect me to ride two thousand miles across scorching desert, my knees spread at a 180-degree angle, perched like a periscope and straddling a piece of black-leather dental floss?"

"You know," Fly says nonchalantly as he digs grease out of his nails with his former toothpick, "a chick over thirty-five has a greater chance of being struck by lightning than landing a man."

Taking a running start, I mount that baby like Roy Rogers.

The last time I was on a Harley, I was twelve years old. Dad bought me a Harley 125cc two-stroke. Basically, it was a Weed Eater with wheels.

Kick-starting it for me, Dad punched her into gear and proceeded to go inside to watch *Bonanza*. He neglected to mention how on earth you stopped the thing.

Every time I passed the den picture window, I would scream bloody murder and Dad would look up, smile, and wave. After wearing a three-foot trench around the house, the thing finally ran out of gas around two A.M.

"How is it?" Sweetie asks, tilting his head back to look up at me over his shoulder.

Maybe it's the altitude or maybe it's the thought of grinding down the pavement at sixty-five miles per hour on my face, but I'm feeling a tad queasy. Motioning with my finger, I manage to get Fly's attention. "By any chance, do you have this seat in a wide?" I whisper into his skull earring.

Fly checks out my derriere. "Try Broyhill."

"It's a lot of money," Sweetie sighs as he finally climbs off.

"It's a fortune," I agree eagerly as I surgically remove myself from the seat and waddle across the room.

I'm thinking that's the end of that, when I notice Sweetie is staring at the Harley like he's watching his life fade away.

Some people say if you love someone, you should protect them from their dreams. If you ever hear me say that, shoot me.

"Then again," I say, throwing Sweetie the checkbook, "what's money to a hog?"

The Car Salesman

According to Sweetie, buying a truck is like dating. If you're not careful, you'll end up paying for that test drive the rest of your life.

"Oh, man," Sweetie's brother Rolex says, "she's a beauty."

"I told you she was hot," Sweetie says.

After kicking tires for six months, Sweetie and Rolex have finally found the truck of their dreams.

"Sweetie," I ponder, "why do men refer to brainless, bloodless, heartless vehicles as females?"

"I can't imagine," Sweetie says dryly.

While the guys circle the truck, a car salesman comes running across the parking lot. This guy's wristwatch weighs more than he does.

"Allu aladule jalaei fkfk," he chirps, handing me his card.

No matter which way I turn it, it looks like an eye exam chart.

"You like truck?" Fez asks, hands folded.

"Could be," Rolex says, playing hard to get.

Apparently, where Fez comes from, "could be" is a done deal.

"We sign papers now," Fez says, heading for his office.

"Whoa!" Rolex says. "Let's not march down the aisle until we've taken her for a spin."

It's Rolex's rule never to buy the cow without getting a

little milk for free. Rolex is single, cute, and owns his own business. Needless to say, he's always got milk.

While the guys are reclining up front, Fez and I are perched on top of those little Chiclets they call seats in the extended cab. With our knees up around our ears, we look like a couple of gargoyles.

"Most plenty room, no?" Fez says, grinning from knee to knee.

"You better put on your seat belt," I say as I buckle up.

"Tkeajiek keakdi ktle dk zimner eirafdke," Fez snorts, rolling his eyes.

"You got that right," Sweetie says as he adjusts his rearview mirror.

"What did he say?" I ask.

"Bossy women come in all colors," Sweetie says.

Throwing her into Drive, Sweetie proceeds to swerve from shoulder to shoulder to check out the steering.

"Uketl tklekrjk jdjkfld, rack and pinion," Fez calls as he ricochets around the cab like a tennis ball.

When we get to a straight stretch in the road, Sweetie floors it. Hearing a little scream, I look over. All I see are a couple of kicking feet sticking through the sliding rear window.

"Most excellent bed liner," Fez yells as I pull him back into the truck.

BAM! BAM! BAM! Sweetie hits a mud puddle, a pothole, and a dip in the road, and BANG! BANG! BANG! Fez hits the roof. Then Sweetie slams on the brakes, and Fez hurls face-first into the headrest like a javelin.

"Most excellent padding, no?" Fez says, head back and pinching his nose to stop the blood.

Finally Sweetie swings into the parking spot and Fez falls out of the truck.

"We sign papers now," he says, stumbling toward his office.

"Stop the organ music, little fellow," Rolex says. "What are you asking for her?"

Frowning, Fez points to the sticker like maybe we'd missed it. Bending down, I take a look and pass out. Our first house didn't cost this much.

"Oh, come on, Fez," Rolex huffs, "I want to buy her, not marry her."

"Yjjdkuant kdlsjflj jdkdks, best price," he says, pointing to the sticker. "You sign papers now."

"Fez, I think we'll check prices on the Internet before we make a commitment," Sweetie says, handing him the keys.

Fez's smile melts. "IN-TER-NET!" he hisses, eyes narrowed.

Rolex checks the exits.

"Fez HATE In-ter-net!" Fez growls.

Slowly, Rolex starts backing up.

"Fez like to BLOW UP In-ter-net!"

Just as Fez throws his arms in the air, his wristwatch goes beep, beep, beep, and Rolex dives for the pavement.

Bending over, Fez stares down at him. "You marry her now?"

"I do," Rolex says.

Topless

"Topless beaches?" Sweetie asks.

"Totally topless," the guy assures him as he fishes the cherry out of his piña colada and plops it in his mouth.

Sweetie and I are at Lord's Castle Resort on the island paradise of Barbados. Lord's Castle is where the British troops stayed when they invaded Grenada. All I can say is, the British sure know how to throw a war.

"The *whole* beach?" Sweetie asks.

"For as far as the eye can see," the guy says, waving his little paper umbrella across the horizon like Mary Poppins.

They call Barbados the air-conditioned island because a constant ten-mile-per-hour breeze blows across your cocoa-buttered body like a GE fan. I have found my higher purpose in life. I am going to become one with my beach chair.

"Sweetie," I say as I drizzle oil all over my body, "how much should I tip the porter for bringing me a bedpan?"

"Totally topless?" Sweetie says.

"Some of them wear sunglasses," the guy says.

And the next thing I know, Sweetie is pushing me onto a plane the size of a hummingbird bound for the French island of Martinique.

As a rule I try not to board airplanes where, prior to take-off, the pilots are crouched under the wing sharing a funny little cigarette.

"Sweetie," I say, nose pressed against the airplane window, "are they doing what I think they're doing?"

"Totally topless," Sweetie says, his pupils shaped into silhouettes of nude women—the kind truck drivers have on their mud flaps.

Twenty minutes late, our pilots finally stumble onto the plane one toke over the line and with a severe case of the munchies.

Other than mowing down a couple of ground-crew guys, takeoff is much smoother than I anticipated. But then one would expect pilots who wear Grateful Dead T-shirts to be adept at getting high. It's the coming-down part that you have to worry about.

It's supposed to be a one-hour jump from Barbados to Martinique. After two hours in the air, Cheech and Chong start flying in a circle and stretching their necks to scan the horizon.

"What are they doing?" I whisper.

"They can't find the island," Sweetie says, suddenly fully alert and leaning forward in his seat.

About this time, Cheech taps on the fuel gauge.

I've never been a whiz at geography, but since we're flying due east—and there's no sign of Africa—I reason we're about to meet our maker.

"Sweetie," I say, taking his hand, "I just want you to know that I love you more than life, and I wouldn't change a thing."

Cupping his hand over mine, Sweetie stares me in the eyes and says, "Our bloodsucking relatives are going to blow every last dime of our money."

On that note, Sweetie and I start tearing the plane apart looking for anything and everything that will float. We just about have the cushions torn out of the seats when Chong jumps up and points out the window.

"Voilà! Martinique!" he cries.

While I'm down on my hands and knees French-kissing the runway, Sweetie flags down an airport security guard.

"*Oui?*" the guard asks, running up to us.

"*Où est le* topless beach?" Sweetie demands.

The guard points with his umbrella and Sweetie takes off.

Glistening with oil and totally topless, Frenchwomen stretch for as far as the eye can see. It's like looking at a griddle full of sunny-side-up eggs at the International House of Pancakes.

No sooner do Sweetie's toes touch sand than a bolt of lightning streaks across the sky. And before you can say *thunder* the entire beach packs up and is gone.

Rain beating down on us, Sweetie and I stare at the empty beach.

"Sweetie, would it help if I took my shirt off and ran around a little?"

"Not totally," Sweetie says, "but it wouldn't hurt."

Le Mower

I don't know why the Pentagon spends so much money on weapons. If you gave every soldier a gas-powered, automatic-feed Weed Eater, total annihilation would just be a matter of time.

It's Saturday morning. Outside, it's so hot and humid, you could steam dumplings just by tossing them into the air. But inside, Mr. Carrier has me chilled to perfection. Feet kicked up and coffee cup in hand, I plan to spend the day getting cozy with a good trashy novel.

"If we hurry," Sweetie says, staring out the window, "we can get the grass mowed before it rains."

"What's this *we* stuff?" I snort.

I never wanted grass. If it were up to me, grass would be like the plague. Except for a couple of seeds preserved in an airtight test tube, you'd have to read about it in books. I like things natural. I figure if God wanted a lawn, He'd mow it.

Sweetie, on the other hand, looks at a meadow and sees chaos. For him, it's like a political thing. A homeowner without grass is teetering on the brink of communism.

After years of skirmishes, we finally divvied up the yard, with the driveway as the demilitarized zone.

On his property, Sweetie hired a bulldozer to scrape off the topsoil. Then he hired a dump truck to dump topsoil back onto it. Then he sowed a hundred pounds of Kentucky blue-grass seed (then sowed it again, after the rain washed it away), fertilized it, watered it, and fogged it with weed killer and insecticide.

Then, of course, he had to buy a John Deere tractor, a Weed Eater, a chain saw, a leaf blower, and a push mower. The only time he actually sets foot on his lawn is to mow it.

Meanwhile, on my property, as long as you stay on the path, you should be okay.

"You wanted the manicured lawn," I say, burying my nose into my book. "You mow it."

On that note, Sweetie buries his nose into my neck and does this little butterfly thing he does with my ear.

"So, tell me again why you dug up a field of wildflowers and planted two acres of grass," I sigh as I lug the lawn mower out of the shed.

"Because AstroTurf was too expensive," he says matter-of-factly as he ties his Rambo red bandanna around his forehead.

The heat factor is 110 degrees and you need a snorkel to keep from drowning in the humidity. Hands on his hips and feet spread, Sweetie takes a deep breath and declares, "I love the smell of DEET in the morning!"

Tucking his pants into his combat boots, Sweetie dons his safety goggles, snake guards, and OSHA-approved sound-dampening earphones.

"YOU'LL BE GLAD YOU DID THIS WHEN IT'S OVER!" he yells. "IT'S GREAT EXERCISE!"

If it were that great, Cindy Crawford would have a lawn-mowing video.

Shimmering in the heat, grass stretches as far as the eye can see. A cloud of mosquitoes hovers overhead like Russian choppers over a rice paddy, and I can hear billions of ticks licking their little lips and tucking in tiny napkins.

We live in the country. A country bug will rip the top off a can of Deep Woods insect repellent, throw a little paper umbrella into it, and slurp it down like a Singapore Sling.

After pushing the mower for around two hours, I stop to refuel. Glancing up, I notice Sweetie heading toward the water garden with his Weed Eater.

Whip, whip, whip, and there goes fifty dollars' worth of spiked rush. Zing! Zing! and my water irises are long gone. I'm just about to faint when I realize Robo Chop is making his way toward the imported lotus.

"No-ooo!" I scream, waving my hands as I take off toward the pond. I make it just in time to watch the last lotus get a crew cut.

"They were encroaching on my turf," Sweetie shrugs.

There was a time when I truly believed world peace was right around the corner. At the moment I'm wondering why they don't sell concertina wire at Home Depot.

Park Place

"There's one!" I say.

Like a compass pointing due north, my finger stays fixed on the empty parking space as Sweetie cruises by.

Sweetie and I are at the mall. For twenty minutes I've been pointing out parking places, and for twenty years he's been ignoring me.

Someone really needs to study why a man will drive for twenty minutes to keep from walking five. I figure it's some sort of leftover from the hunter-gatherer society. Nowadays, Man hunts parking places and Woman gathers garments at the Gap.

"Why don't we park over there?" I ask, pointing to the acres of empty spaces on the other side of the median.

"Oh, sure, we could park there," Sweetie huffs, "if you never want to see the truck again."

Let's review. We're driving a 1985 Ford pickup. The tailgate is held up with bungee cords, the driver's door is kicked in, and the passenger-side rearview mirror has an erection problem. It just hangs there.

Needless to say, securing the vehicle with The Club is not a high priority.

Suddenly Sweetie floors it and my neck snaps like a wishbone. Zipping up one row, then down the next, Sweetie skids to a stop just as a woman loaded down with shopping bags arrives at her gray Honda Accord.

Shuffling her bags from one arm to the other, the woman scratches through her purse. Just when it looks like she's found her keys, she pulls out the remains of a Pop-Tart. Studying it, she takes a hairy bite, then drops it back into her purse.

Finally locating her key ring, she sticks a key in the car door. After fidgeting forever, she pulls the key out, looks at it, and frowns. Leaning back, she looks at the car. Then, hand shading her eyes, she peeks inside.

Hefting her shopping bags, the woman walks around to the gray Nissan parked next to her.

Rolling his narrowed eyes in my direction, Sweetie glares at me like I'm decked out in fig leaves with a half-eaten apple in my hand.

"Hey!" I say defensively. "I have never done that in my life!"

I'm referring, of course, to eating a raw Pop-Tart.

Meanwhile, having dropped her keys back in her purse, the woman is digging like a gopher again.

Sweetie lights a cigarette.

Door finally open, the woman tosses her bags into the backseat and climbs in. Then begins the pre-flight inspection. Lock door. Buckle seat belt. Adjust radio. Check makeup in rearview mirror. Check makeup again.

When she takes out the lipstick, Sweetie explodes. "Good Gawd, woman!" he thunders at the windshield. "You have the rear end of an eighteen-wheeler! Your dentist doesn't even know you have lips!"

Finally the woman's brake lights blink and she starts jerking back out of her parking space.

Nostrils flaring, Sweetie puts the truck in first and revs the engine.

She backs up. Stops. Looks both ways.

Backs up. Stops. Looks both ways.

Temples pounding, Sweetie grips the steering wheel until his knuckles crack.

Suddenly the woman slams on her brakes in the middle of the road. Tilting her rearview, she checks her teeth for Pop-Tart crumbs.

While Sweetie is banging his head against the steering wheel, the woman putters off and a red Mustang zings around the corner and slingshots into our parking space.

"Why did we come to the mall?" I ask, eyes straight ahead.

"To walk," Sweetie says.

I wonder if anyone has studied the cardiac workout a guy gets from parking a car.

Our Nation's Synthetic Resources

"A woman's size doesn't mean a thing to me," Howard says.

Heads swiveling in unison, Doc and Sweetie do an involuntary scan of Howard's wife, Jane. When a guy tells you chest size doesn't matter, you can bet his wife is flat as an airport runway.

We're having this intellectual conversation at a restaurant while waiting for our friend Betty to arrive. The candles are lit and champagne is chilling in the bucket. Betty just had breast augmentation, and tonight we're celebrating their first public appearance.

"The mammary gland is purely functional," Doc states clinically, "a biological necessity, and should be viewed as such."

This comment has *gynecologist* written all over it.

"They're fat sacks," Sweetie interjects while crunching on a bread stick. "What difference does it make how fat they are?"

What can I tell you? It was Sweetie's poetic way with words that swept me off my feet.

Back in high school, all the girls used to take the pencil test. If your chest couldn't hold a pencil up—without using your hands—you could get away with going braless. Betty could hold up a jumbo box of Crayola crayons. She didn't need a bra; she needed a crane. But after nursing two kids, the fizz seemed to go out of Betty's champagne.

After much soul-searching and a personal loan from the teachers' credit union, Betty decided to reinflate her ego. And whether the guys are willing to admit it or not, they're bouncing up and down to see the results.

"So," Jane says, "you guys see no need for a woman to enlarge her breasts?"

"It's a waste of our nation's synthetic resources," Sweetie states with complete authority.

About this time, we get a side view of Betty through the window as she walks down the sidewalk. A hush falls over the table.

Howard misses his mouth with his fork and almost stabs Sweetie. Sweetie doesn't notice. Eyes glued on Betty, he feels his soul leave his body and take his brain with it.

"Throw the golf balls away, boys!" Doc whistles. "Tonight we're shootin' baskets!"

By the end of the meal, the federal government has declared the pool of drool under our table a wetland and is stocking it with largemouth bass.

Of course this doesn't bother Jane, Leila, or me a bit.

"What do men need women for?" Jane hisses as soon as the ladies' room door creaks to a close. "Just give a guy a plastic blow-up doll. He'll never know the difference!"

The three of us are standing at the sinks in front of the mirror, dejectedly checking our, uh, makeup.

"Are we people or are we poodles?!" Jane continues to rant as she fogs herself with CK. "I'm not getting my tail trimmed or my chest poofed for any man!"

"What's important is the perfection of the mind and soul," Leila insists, "to find inner peace and to fulfill one's highest purpose."

The door opens and Betty bounces in. I don't know how peaceful she's feeling, but if her purpose gets any higher they're going to suffocate her.

Taking the turn a little sharp, Betty's implants slam into the towel holder and knock it off the wall. I guess it's like learning to park a Cadillac after you've been puttering around in a Volkswagen.

"Did you hurt them?" I ask as a wall tile crashes to the floor.

"Nah," Betty says, thumping them like melons. "They're like a rock."

"You're not wearing a bra!" Jane says incredulously.

"Nope," Betty quips. "These babies are totally self-supporting."

"Does it bother you that they're fake?" Leila asks, leaning forward and squinting like she expects to see bolts sticking out.

Betty gives this some thought. "It's kind of like a car," she says thoughtfully. "You'd rather have leather upholstery, but in the long run, vinyl doesn't affect the performance."

Dress

According to Sweetie, the reason there has never been a female president is because wars have been fought and won in less time than it takes a woman to pull on a pair of panty hose.

"Are you shearing sheep up there?" he yells.

"It's summer," I yell back down. "I'm picking cotton!"

Men have no sympathy. The fact is, a guy could tattoo a gray suit on his body, and, except for the tie, be appropriately dressed for everything from a wedding to a wake.

But a woman has it tough. Not only does she have to dress for the occasion, she also has to wear a color that doesn't make her skin look like rigor mortis has set in and yet is seasonally appropriate. She has to dress to conceal some bulges, yet dress to enhance others.

If she overdresses, people think she's a snob. If she underdresses, people still think she's a snob.

If a woman dresses too old, she's dowdy. If she dresses too young, she's a slut. If she dresses too conservative, she's a prude. If she dresses too provocative, she's a slut. If she wears dark colors, she's drab. If she wears bright colors . . .

You start to see the pattern here.

All in all, it takes less decision making to launch a satellite. But the hardest part of getting dressed is trying to please the man in your life.

When Sweetie and I first started dating I could throw on a pair of cutoffs and a couple of Band-Aids and he was tickled pink. But the minute we became "attached," he hammered a flag in my navel, staked his claim on me as his private property, and declared, "The only time I want to see *that* swimsuit wet is when you're pulling it out of the washer!"

Nowadays, it would take a heat-seeking missile to find any flesh on this body. Suddenly, I'm shopping at stores like Nuns Are Us and Chastity Threads.

But if covering up from my nose to my toes was all there was to it, I wouldn't have a problem. The fact is, I have a better chance at achieving world peace than dressing to please Sweetie—especially when he has to entertain an important client.

"You're not wearing *that*, are you?" he says.

"No, of course not," I say. "This is totally inappropriate beee-caaause . . . " I pause, motioning with my hand for him to finish the sentence.

". . . because every time I look at you, I feel like I'm taking the Rorschach test. Think solids."

"Absolutely," I say.

I thunder back up the stairs, jerk off the dress I spent three days shopping for and half my paycheck on, and, after tearing through my closet, settle on a nice three-piece suit that requires changing hose, shoes, and accessories. Throwing it all on, I run back downstairs.

Sweetie closes his eyes and shakes his head. "If you had a mole with a black hair sticking out, you'd look just like my ninth-grade English teacher," he says.

Exactly the aura every girl dreams of exuding.

"Okay," I say. "Help me out here. What am I aiming for?"

"Oh, you know . . . conservative, without concealing the fact that you're a woman. Sophisticated, yet playful. Worldly, but Made in America."

"Kind of Sharon Stone dipped in Jackie O., with a Sandra Day O'Connor on the side," I say. "Piece of cake." I fly back up the stairs.

Four wardrobe changes later, I'm wearing a simple black dress and looking like an Italian widow from *The Godfather*.

"You're wearing too much blush," he says, scanning me for defects.

"It isn't blush," I gasp. "I'm having a heart attack."

"Well," he says, pushing me out the door, "try not to croak before dessert."

The Island

"Okay," Allison says, clinking her cup with a spoon. "Question number one . . ."

Al runs the family business. Coffee at her condo always comes with a mission statement.

"You're marooned on a tropical island with one person," Al says. "Who would it be?"

Rosie, Maxine, and I kick back, and in a matter of seconds, seagulls are crying around the track lights and the trade winds are melting the grease on Al's Jenn-Air.

We girls are great at visualization. It's the implementation we can't seem to get a handle on.

The warm foaming surf washes against the white sandy shore. Palm trees sway in the breeze. Closing my eyes, I feel the hot sun on my tanned, cellulite-free body.

Suddenly, the beach is swarming with bronzed half-naked Sports Illustrated *swimsuit models! Gasping, I zap them into penguins and send them—flippers flapping—waddling off toward the Playboy Mansion in Antarctica.*

Meanwhile, leaning against a palm tree, body taut and glistening with a sheen of sweat from the heat, is . . .

". . . Bob Vila," Maxine says.

"That pudgy little guy from *This Old House?*" Al asks. "You can have anyone in the world, and you choose a Pillsbury Doughboy with a tool belt?"

"Hey!" Max snaps. "I bet our hut doesn't leak."

" . . . Martha Stewart," Rosie sighs dreamily.

Rolling our raised eyebrows at each other, we all decide to leave this one in Rosie's well-organized closet.

"I'd choose Woody Allen," Al says as she burps a cappuccino from her fifteen-hundred-dollar espresso maker. "He's talented, intelligent, funny . . . "

Maxine sticks her finger down her throat. "That wrinkled little Rumpelstiltskin would whine you to death in a month."

Of course there's only one person I'd take for a tumble in the tide. Sweetie.

It's my philosophy that if the guy you're with isn't the guy you want to spend *From Here to Eternity* with, you're with the wrong guy.

"Well?" Al demands, staring at me.

"George Clooney," I say.

Of course, I do have a reputation to uphold.

"The *actor?*" Al gags. "Somebody shove me into shallow water."

"If a pop-top can of sardines washed ashore," Max huffs, "that boy wouldn't know what to do with it."

"You are aware that he has a pet pig." Rosie frowns.

While Al, Max, and Rosie continue to tear poor George to pieces, I catch a steamer back to the island.

Passionately wrapped in each other's arms, Sweetie and I roll on the white sand, totally oblivious of the foaming tide that is washing over us.

"Sweetie," I say, coming up for air, "aren't you a little warm in your three-piece suit, black socks, and Rockports?"

"You know how I hate the feel of sand between my toes," Sweetie says.

Meanwhile, back at our hut, Woody Allen is wringing his hands and whining about the danger of getting skin cancer this close to the equator, Martha Stewart is throwing a fit because there's simply no way she can prepare a decent conch chowder in such a poorly equipped kitchen, and Bob Vila, clipboard in hand, is trying to explain why the new grass roof cost twice as much as the estimate.

Voodoo

Weston's new housekeeper is from the islands. She dances barefoot, has skin the color of café au lait, and speaks with an accent as thick as rum. It goes without saying—dust removal is not her greatest asset.

"So," Marjie says, throwing a long brown leg over the arm of Weston's wingback, "you be Monsieur Wes-stone's *bon ami.*"

"*Bon ami,* that's French for good friend," Weston says as he shoves a pile of clothes over on the couch so Sweetie can sit down.

"Oh, yeah," Sweetie says, kicking his feet up. "The *bon*-nest."

And getting *bon*-ner by the minute, judging by Sweetie's smitten smile.

I practically have to hog-tie Sweetie to get him to have dinner at Weston's. But introduce him to a girl with an accent, and he starts thinking time-share.

"Anyone want something to drink?" Wes asks as he reaches under the couch to scrounge up a couple of dirty glasses.

Normally, Weston's condo is so neat you can eat off the Jacuzzi. Tonight, I'm a little worried about touching the doorknobs.

"Dinner will be ready in just a minute," Wes says as he ties on an apron.

"Whatyu be havin'?" Marjie asks as she twirls the ever-stylish chicken's claw that's tied around her neck.

"Your favorite," Wes assures her as he heads toward the kitchen.

She doesn't cook. She doesn't clean. And she doesn't do laundry. Leave it to Weston to hire a trophy housekeeper.

Meanwhile, Marjie, bracelets jangling and reeking of Panama Jack, is reading Sweetie's palm.

"Rich folk always be talkin' 'bout what was. And middle-class folk always talkin' 'bout what gonna be. Marjie, the praline she melt on the tongue."

"That means she lives for the moment," Weston says, dropping a tray of half-frozen shrimp egg rolls on the coffee table.

I can see why Weston is so taken with her. He's a lawyer. Mumbo jumbo is his life.

". . . but sometimes," Marjie whispers, "Marjie see what will be."

Marjie bends over Sweetie's hand and you can practically hear the voodoo drums. "D'yu no work with the hands," she says, tracing a lily-white wrinkle with her fingernail.

"That's right!" Sweetie says.

Marjie rubs and rubs Sweetie's hand, tracing the lines.

"I don't suppose you read any other body parts?" Sweetie asks.

"Hmmm," Marjie hums.

"What?" Sweetie asks, looking down at his hand.

"Monsieur Sweetie used to be . . . how d'yu say . . . a real stud."

"Used to be?" Sweetie frowns.

"Now, Monsieur Sweetie, he be work, work, work," Marjie says, shaking her head.

"Work, work, work," Sweetie echoes like a parrot.

"Oh, *mon dieu!*" Marjie says, eyes rolling back and body writhing. "*Marjie see what will be!*"

Mouths gaping, Sweetie and Weston stare like zombies as Marjie starts dancing around the room.

Bare feet stomping and dreadlocks tossing, Marjie moans and groans as she twirls and gyrates around Weston's new entertainment center.

The egg rolls thaw and the walls start to sweat.

Suddenly, eyes rolled back in her head and mouth gaping, Marjie lets out a bloodcurdling scream and drops onto the chair as if she's been shot.

"Incredible! Amazing!" the guys shout as they give Marjie a standing ovation.

Sighing, she reaches for an egg roll and kicks her feet back up.

"Well?" I finally ask. "What is Sweetie's future?"

"Pretty much the same old thing." Marjie shrugs.

The Man Not Taken

Two roads diverged in a yellow wood . . . and Teddy climbed into his BMW and headed for the mall.

"Windemere Estates is *the* place to live," Ted says, drawing quotation marks in the air and bobbing his head like Richard Nixon.

Back when Sweetie, Philo, and Ted were in college, *the* place to live was the back of a VW van. They were going to bring peace to the world. And in his own way, Teddy has. You know that little hologram of a dove on your credit card? That's Teddy.

Ted's new neighborhood is one of those high-security zero-lot-line gated communities. I thought the guard was going to strip-search me before he'd let me in.

"That's Carlos," the woman from next door says. "Did he pat you down?"

"Pat me down?"

"Well . . ."—she smiles knowingly—"maybe next time."

Somehow, I doubt Patty Cakes has ever seen the back of a van. The only reason she was born with a silver spoon in her mouth was because the gold-plated silverware was being polished at the time.

"Imported Italian granite," Ted brags to Patty as he runs his hand over his new bar. "From the same mine as Mussolini's mausoleum."

Nothing quite demonstrates the superiority of a free economy like dipping a chip on a dictator's tomb.

Judging by the way Teddy's been strutting his stuff in front of Patty all night, he has high hopes of negotiating a corporate merger. Judging by the way Patty's sitting on the bar stool, she's open to a takeover.

"Found my bathtub in a field," Philo says, stroking his beard. "The neighbor was using it as a watering trough for his hogs."

"You stole your bathtub?" Patty says incredulously as she licks an olive like a lollipop.

"He was looking for something better anyway." Philo shrugs.

While the rest of us let our ideals slide with the interest rates, Philo held fast. His idea of keeping up with the Joneses is having a recent issue of *Mother Jones* magazine by the toilet.

"Philo lives in a barn," Ted says as he clinks ice cubes (made from Perrier) into the glasses.

"You mean a barn . . . like with stalls?" one of Ted's new neighbors asks, flabbergasted.

If this guy arches his eyebrows any higher, he'll be able to drop his membership at the Hair Club for Men.

Not only did Philo choose the road less traveled, he chose the road still under construction. There isn't a board in his barn that doesn't have PROPERTY OF THE U.S. GOVERNMENT stamped on it.

Ted presses a button and the curtains automatically open to a panoramic view of Patty's Jacuzzi. These houses are so close together, you can count your neighbor's nose hairs, especially with Teddy's X2000 telescope.

"My nearest neighbor's a mile down the road," Philo says, bending down to take a tour of the neighborhood through the telescope. "I can stand on my front porch buck naked and take a whiz over the rail."

This pretty much snuffs out the conversation like a fire hose.

Clearing her throat, Patty finally breaks the silence. "I'd love to see your barn sometime," she says.

"Honey," Philo says, "*you* couldn't get there from here."

"Spinach risotto?" Ted asks, anxiously aiming a platter at Patty.

"I'm very good at directions," Patty says as her French-manicured fingers do the walking up the holes of Philo's Levi's.

"Tell me one thing you believe in," Philo says, grabbing her hand.

Philo may be cheap, but he's not easy.

Slowly, licking her lacquered lips, Patty gives this some thought. "Freedom's just another word for trust fund," she says.

"Good enough," Philo says, grabbing her arm and heading for his van.

Two roads diverged . . .

Glancing back over her shoulder, Patty blows Teddy a kiss.

. . . and apparently, Patty plans to burn rubber down them both.

Carpe Diem

People used to say kids should be seen and not heard. What do we need to see them for? I say we leave them in day care until they're old enough to vote.

I'm draped in a towel and lying on a redwood bench in Leila's steam room. It's warm and wet, and the only noise is an occasional hiss of steam. All that's missing is a six-foot Swede named Sven kneading my body like I'm bread dough.

You can have your pearly gates. When I die, drop me off at a Turkish bath.

I am well on my way to dissolving when there's a click and the door opens. The steam swirls and the door closes.

Slowly my invader materializes in the fog. His spindly arms dangle from his hairless little body to his knobby knees, and his skin is so white he glows. It's like looking at an alien autopsy.

"That's my place," Leila's thirteen-year-old kid says.

"Why aren't you in school?"

"Mom says I'm sick," he says.

"How can she tell?" I ask.

They don't make kids like they used to. In my day, as long as we weren't bleeding on the floor, Mom threw us on the bus.

"It's my place," he says, "and it's my house."

This might have carried more clout if his voice hadn't cracked like Minnie Mouse.

"Still dating those Victoria's Secret catalogues?" I ask dryly.

Eyes the size of flying saucers, E.T. gasps. All of a sudden, his little body goes limp and he starts wheezing like Darth Vader. Frantically fumbling through his pockets, he finally takes out his asthma inhaler and sprays a few shots into his mouth.

"Are you okay?" I ask, sitting up.

E.T.'s lips are turning blue and his breathing sounds like a death rattle. Gripping my towel, I jump down off the bench. My hand's on the door handle when E.T. makes a mad dash for my place.

"Ain't gonna happen," I say, blocking him with my body.

Looking up at me, he narrows his alien eyes and shoots me with laser hate beams. Then, swiveling around, he pads over to the bench across from me. Holding on to the elastic waist-band of his swimming trunks for dear life, he hops up onto the shelf and resumes glaring at me.

Closing my eyes, I drift off. Sven has just about got the kinks out of my shoulders and is drizzling oil on my back when I hear beeping. Cracking my eyes open, I see E.T. pulling a tiny cellular phone out of the pocket of his trunks.

I'm hoping it's the Mother Ship telling him to beam back up.

"On-line," he answers. Deep in concentration, E.T. bites his nails while he rolls and unrolls his toes. He may have a body like a rubber chicken, but he could play Rachmaninoff with those feet.

After around fifteen minutes of teenage chatter, I've had all I can take. "Hey!" I snap. "E.T., phone home somewhere else."

"I gotta go," he mutters, hand cupped over the phone.

Pushing the antenna down, he slides the phone back into his pocket. Kicking his feet, he resumes glaring at me.

"You're a woman, right?" he suddenly asks out of the foggy blue.

My theory is, if a guy has to ask, the answer probably isn't going to do him any good.

"See, I met this girl in a chat room on the Internet," he says, watching his toes flex, ". . . and well, she wants to, like, meet . . . like, in person."

"Human contact," I say. "Don't you think that's pushing it a bit?"

"See, that's what I think," he says. "I mean, like, we've only been e-mailing a couple of months."

"Why rush it?" I say. "You've got your whole life ahead of you."

"Right," he says, bobbing his head up and down.

"Then again," I add, "you don't look so good. You might not be around that long. And you know what they say: carpe diem—seize the day."

Chewing his nail, E.T. gives this some thought. "You got anything on under that towel?"

Ma Bell

The phone is ringing and I can't find it.

"Sweetie!" I yell as I scratch through his piles of papers on the table, "Where's the phone?"

Normally I'm not the kind of girl who goes into a frenzy over a ringing phone. In fact I've actually been known to let it ring. But I'm expecting an important call, and have been waiting for it all day.

On ring two, I run into the living room and dive into Sweetie's stacks of stuff on the couch.

"Sweetie!" I scream, tossing his dirty shirts over my shoulder. "Where's the phone?"

On ring three, I climb over the crates of files, wedge past the cases of printing paper, and crawl under the web of computer, printer, and fax machine cables to Sweetie's desk.

When one is trying to find the phone on Sweetie's desk, it's best to approach it like an archaeological dig. When you get to the mail dated before Alexander Graham Bell invented the telephone, you might as well dig elsewhere.

On ring four, I give up ever seeing the portable phone again. Racing upstairs, I slide across the hardwood floor, do a one-and-a-half gainer onto Sweetie's lap, and grab the receiver on the upstairs phone.

"Hello!"

Dial tone.

Sweetie stares down at me from over his crumpled newspaper. "I don't answer the phone after four-thirty," he says, "and I make more money than you."

Arching up, I reach underneath me and pull out the instrument of pain that's stabbing me in the back. It's the portable phone.

"A *lot* more money," Sweetie says.

A woman's relationship with the telephone is fairly simple. If Ma Bell had phones that changed the oil in the car, there would be no need for men.

"Sweetie," I say as I count my cracked ribs, "you're going to miss me when I run off with Richard Gere."

"They have phones in Tibet?" he asks, sticking his face back into the paper.

When it comes to telephones, there are two kinds of guys. Guys who can't get enough phone and guys like Sweetie, who think talking to a chick on the phone would be great if he could just turn the sound off.

Phone Guy gives great phone. He calls to make sure you got home okay. He calls to let you know he's thinking of you. He calls just to hear your voice.

Phone Phobia Guy thinks Phone Guy is gay.

About this time, the phone rings.

"I'm not here," Sweetie grumbles from behind the paper.

"Oh, hi, Mother," I say, snuggling back and kicking my feet up. "It's your mother," I say, hand over the receiver.

"*I'm not here!*" Sweetie pantomimes while shaking his head and waving his hands.

"I'm great . . . work's great . . . Sweetie's great . . . Yeah, he's sitting right here. Wanna talk to him?"

Sweetie scowls at me like I'm the crud you clean out of the bathtub drain. Seeing no way out, he jerks the phone away from me. "Hi, Mom," he says. "I'm great . . . work's great . . . she's great."

Sweetie is in pain. As far as he's concerned, making small

talk on the phone is right up there with bamboo shoots under the fingernails.

"Look, Mom," Sweetie suddenly says, "I've gotta go . . . uh-huh . . . Yeah, I know we never talk. Well, I would call more, but *she* won't let me."

Sweetie hands me the phone. "Mom wants to talk to you."

Warming the Bench

"Oh, my Gawd!" Nancy cries as she slaps her cheeks. "Sweetie looks just like Paul Newman!"

After I recover from snorting a three-dollar cup of coffee through my nose, I swivel my head—along with everyone else in the restaurant—and take a long hard look at Sweetie.

"Girlfriend," I say, "you've been warming the bench too long."

Being a single mom, Nancy's been out of the game a while. And, as everyone knows, if a girl doesn't shag a few balls every now and then, all the senses start to go. I give Nancy six months, and she'll need a Seeing Eye dog.

Sweetie and I are "doing lunch" in the Big Apple. Nancy brought us to one of those restaurants where the beautiful people don't actually eat, they just order food—then pose with their forks in the air. Occasionally a cell phone rings and some emaciated model gets confused and rams fat-free pasta up her ear.

"It's his attitude," Nancy says as she continues to study Sweetie with her fork in the air. "He has that edgy attitude that drives women wild."

In my red-neck of the woods, Sweetie's "edgy attitude" is called "having a nicotine fit."

When Sweetie figured out he had developed a twenty-five-hundred-dollar-a-year cigarette habit, he hung up his Bic.

51

Sweetie may blow smoke in the face of death, but he's not about to watch his money go up in flames.

Needless to say, his system went into shock. Every so often I hold a mirror under his nose to see if he's still breathing. Otherwise, he's taking it pretty well. I, on the other hand, am mean as a snake.

"In order to quit cold turkey," I explain as I reach across the table and spear whatever it is Nancy's not eating, "he had to give up everything that he associates with smoking."

"You don't mean . . ." Nancy says, eyebrows lifted.

"*Everything.*" I nod.

"Then I take it your bench is warm?"

"Sweetie won't even let me pick up the bat," I say as I spit a foreign object into my napkin. I'm thinking it's the remains of our centerpiece. My eyesight is fading so fast, I can't be sure.

Sweetie suddenly twitches for the first time in weeks. Sliding his chair back, he stands up.

"I'll be back," he says from behind his aviator sunglasses.

The last time we see Sweetie, he's standing on the sidewalk, staring up at a fifty-foot billboard of Broadway dancers wearing nothing but Calvin Klein underwear.

Our Ethiopian waiter shows up with the dessert tray, and I can't believe my eyes. "Oh, my Gawd!" I cry, slapping my cheeks. "Our waiter looks just like Brad Pitt!"

"Here, honey," Nancy says, handing me her bottled ice water, "pour this in your lap."

When Sweetie finally comes back to the table, he makes Cool Hand Luke look like a nerd with pocket protectors. Every woman in the place is checking the boy out. There's pep in Sweetie's step, and if he were packing any more lead in his pencil the NYPD would throw him against a car and frisk him.

"I take it you scored," Nancy says, pretending to take a sip of cappuccino.

"Four dollars a pack," Sweetie says, tapping his pocket. "A deal at twice the price."

"Excuse me," the woman at the table next to us purrs, "but do you have a cigarette?"

With James Bond panache, Sweetie taps the fresh pack on the back of his hand and offers her the extended cigarettes.

"Oh, you saved my life!" she oozes. Then, reaching with both hands, she proceeds to help herself to half the pack.

"Sweetie," I say, patting the tablecloth, "I can't see."

"Don't worry," Sweetie says. "The Miracle Worker is back."

Cultured Chicks

I think the exact moment Sweetie figured out he was dating a cultural void was on our second date. He was waxing eloquent about Michelangelo, and I said with total assurance, "Frankly, I think Budweiser is just as good for the money."

"Gimme two tickets to Jesse Jackson," I tell the girl at the box office as I dig through my knapsack.

"Reverend Jesse Jackson?" She frowns. "Don't you mean Jessye Norman?"

"Whichever one sings," I say, with an exasperated flip of the hand.

Sweetie was a music major. Half the time I have no idea what he's talking about, but for some reason it never fails to make me want to tear his clothes off and sing high C.

"There aren't many tickets left," the ticket girl says, staring at her computer screen.

"To hear an opera singer?" I ask incredulously.

"Well, Jessye Norman is the best singer in the world."

"Let's hear her sing the theme song to the *Titanic*," I huff, "then we'll talk."

The truth is, I worry that someday Sweetie will be torn between a woman who shares his passion for the arts—and my passion for pork chops. And so I am determined to get cultured.

"Pretty good seats, huh?" I chitchat with the guy next to me.

"People in the know," he sniffs, not looking up from his program, "sit on the left side of the theater."

"Then why are you sitting here?"

"I date the lead cellist."

"Hubba hubba," I say, jabbing my elbow into his cummerbund.

"You're looking at the viola section," he says dryly.

Artsy types get very snappish when you underestimate the size of their companion's instrument.

"Piano player," I say smugly, throwing my thumb in Sweetie's direction.

"Hubba hubba," the guy says.

Listening to Mozart may raise your IQ, but nobody puts you to sleep like Schubert. By intermission, I'm snoring.

The second half gets off to a better start. I actually recognize some of the music and, in the fever of the moment, can't help but quietly sing along. "Kill da wabbit . . . Kill da wabbit . . ."

Finally, silk robe fluttering like wings, Jessye Norman regally promenades onto the stage. They call her Diva, and that's an understatement. With her hair swept up and a gold scarf wound around like a crown, she's a walking Statue of Liberty.

Taking his place beside her, the skinny little conductor looks like Jiminey Cricket in a tuxedo. Under normal circumstances, this guy couldn't cast a shadow if he were waving an open umbrella, but the minute he taps his baton on the music stand, he turns into the Tasmanian Devil. White hair sticking out in all directions and tuxedo tails flapping, he spins his stick arms like propellers and tears around the podium so fast, all you can see is his exhaust.

Stretching their necks, every coifed head on our side of

the theater leans to the right . . . leans to the left . . . raises up out of their seats . . . then makes a dive for the right again. It's like we're dancing "Walk like an Egyptian" to Wagner.

Meanwhile, all we can see of Ms. Norman are bits and pieces that blink in and out of sight like she's singing in a strobe light.

If I'd had the foresight to wear waterproof mascara, I would cry. A cultured chick would have known to get seats on the left side of the theater. Face burning, I glance over at Sweetie.

Eyes closed and face lifted, he leans forward in his lousy seat as though he is being kissed. Somehow, I suspect that Sweetie can see Jessye Norman more clearly than anyone in the room. "To hear a voice like that," Sweetie whispers reverently, "may only come once in a lifetime."

"Yeah," I say, "and I hear she's a heck of a preacher."

The Truck Stop

"There's just somethin' 'bout that song," Loretta sighs as she wipes the Formica countertop in front of us, "that makes a girl want to climb into a pickup truck and test that baby's shocks."

It's Monday night at the Truck Stop. Garth Brooks is on the jukebox, and truckers, one eye on the weather station and the other eye on Loretta, are curled around their meat and three.

"Number 576!" a voice reverberates over the intercom. "Your shower is ready!"

Licking her thumb, Loretta counts her tips, then stuffs them in her pocket. Loretta and I have been friends since Mr. Norfleet's high school history class. I guided her through the Louisiana Purchase, and she guided me through my first Frederick's of Hollywood purchase.

"This job is just temporary," Loretta assures Sweetie as she grabs our burgers from the pickup window and slides them in front of us. "Just 'til I get my business goin' again."

Currently, Loretta is in need of a little financial advice, and so I am lending her Sweetie.

"What happened to your business?" Sweetie asks, peeking under his bun.

"I guess you could call it a hostile takeover." Knocking the cap off a Coke on the counter, Loretta hands it to Sweetie.

"My scum-suckin' ex-husband got it in the divorce. Mama always said that boy was a gold digger."

"What kind of business was it?" Sweetie asks, wiping the top of the bottle on the only clean surface he can find—his shirt.

"Window washin'."

"So your ex-husband got all the . . ."

"Buckets, squeegees . . . the whole kit and caboodle."

Flipping open her stainless steel lighter, Loretta fires up a menthol. Closing the lighter with a snap, she drops it back into her apron. At the Truck Stop, the smoking section is anywhere you can't smell gas.

"But I've learned my lesson," Loretta says, blowing smoke toward the greasy acoustic tile ceiling. "No more investors. From now on, this girl is strictly privately held."

"I'd like to privately hold you, Loretta," a trucker down the bar calls out.

"Honey," Loretta huffs, "you couldn't handle it."

"Woof! Woof! Woof!" the other truckers howl.

Resting her chin in hands, Loretta leans down on the counter in front of Sweetie. "I went to the bank to try and borrow the money," she says. "But that banker man wants me to put up my Z-28 Camaro for a two-thousand-dollar loan!"

"Bankers are nothing but Mafia in cheap suits," Sweetie says, smacking the bottom of the catsup bottle over his fries.

"I told him, 'Mister, take a look at these roots. Underneath this blond exterior is the brunette brain of a businesswoman.' "

Bending over, Loretta points to the top of her head. Sweetie's eyes never quite make it to her roots. Transfixed by the cross swinging back and forth in her cleavage, Sweetie appears to be having a religious experience.

"I hope that banker gets fleas in his shorts," Loretta sniffs.

"And may they multiply like compounding interest," Sweetie adds.

"So," Loretta says, flicking her spent cigarette into the dishwater, "what should I do?"

"Let me take a look at your financial situation," Sweetie says, crunching into a catsup-covered fry, "and we'll go from there."

Head cocked, Loretta studies Sweetie. "Come here," she says, motioning with her finger.

Like a newborn chick, Sweetie leans across the counter and Loretta meets him halfway. Closing her eyes, Loretta sticks out her tongue and slowly licks a drip of catsup off Sweetie's chin.

"Think of it as your retainer," she says throatily.

"Loretta," I warn, "Sweetie is privately held."

"Just primin' that pump for you, honey," Loretta says to me with a wink.

Something tells me this is how hostile takeovers begin.

Koi-tus

"We don't have time to fool around," Sweetie says. "Get it in . . . and get it out."

Sweetie and I are sitting in the parking lot of the water garden nursery. I just spent four hours in three stores watching him smell, feel, and roll on every floor mat the auto industry has to offer. Now I'm in the mood for a little shopping, and he tells me we only have time for a quickie.

"Get it in," he says, "and get it out."

"Have we had this discussion before"—I frown—". . . because this sure seems familiar?"

Throwing his arm in the air, Sweetie starts timing me.

Running around the water reeds and bulrushes, I finally spot a tanned girl wearing shorts and standing knee-deep in tropical water lilies.

"Water hyacinths," I wheeze midstride.

The girl points and I keep on truckin'.

Rounding a corner, I almost trip over half a dozen women sitting around an artificial waterfall. Their legs are crossed in the lotus position and they each have one hand dangling in a koi fish pond.

"Ooooh. Aaaaah," they chant, with blissful expressions on their faces.

Opening her eyes, one of the women motions for me to join them. Remembering my "in and out" promise to Sweetie,

I hesitate. Then I rationalize that if I can grow old waiting for him to shop for floor mats, surely he can give me five minutes to browse for enlightenment.

I couldn't get my body into a full lotus with a crowbar, but I plop down on the grass and fold my thunder thighs the best I can.

Without further instruction, the woman dips her hand back in the pool, closes her eyes, and resumes moaning.

Leaning over the water, I take a peek at the koi. They're the size of baby porpoises, their fluorescent colors will blind you, and they have mouths as wide as dinner plates. If Mick Jagger was a fish, he'd be a koi.

From across the crowded pond, a black-and-gold koi makes fish-eye contact with me. I don't know, maybe it's the way his scales glitter in the sunlight. Or maybe I'm just a sucker for the slimy silent type. Whatever the reason, I decide to take a chance. Cautiously, I dip my hand in the water.

Teasing me with a little fishplay, the koi swims around and around, giving my hand a whirlpool massage. Then suddenly, without warning, his feathery fins brush against my skin.

"Oh," I gasp, chill bumps running up one arm and down the other.

Brazenly he rubs the entire length of his body across my hand, like he's a cat. Forget the lotus position. I'm so limp, you could twirl me around a fork like angel-hair pasta.

Then, after a few nibbles on my palm, he takes my finger in his fish mouth and starts sucking on it.

"Ohhh, sushi!" I shudder, sucking in a breath.

Okay, so maybe he thinks I'm a worm. I'm of the school a little role-playing adds spice to a relationship.

About this time, Sweetie charges up, catching me in the act. "I've been waiting for you for twenty minutes!" he blasts. "Do you intend to buy that fish or not?"

"Buy him?" I huff. "I'm going to marry him!"

Tax Man

"A word of advice," the tax auditor says as he strolls into Sweetie's office, "the fish is killed by its open mouth."

"Confucius?" I ask.

"Mafia Handbook," he says.

Leave it to Sweetie and me to get audited by Vito, the Mafia Tax Man.

Casually taking a look around the room, the Tax Man suddenly pulls out a flashlight and takes a peek under Sweetie's desk.

"Old habits are hard to break," he says as he climbs up on a chair.

"Old habits?" I ask, frowning up at him.

"Used to own an exterminating business," he says as he drives a pen knife into an exposed beam.

An exterminator on the IRS fast track. We're doomed.

"So," Tax Man says, dusting his hands off and dropping into a chair, "are you nervous about the audit?"

"Should we be?" I ask.

"Well, you know what they say," he says as he pops the lock on his briefcase. "Make a mistake with the Mafia, you wake up with a horse head in your bed. Make a mistake with the IRS, you wake up without a bed."

I make a note to put the bed in my mother's name.

Meanwhile, Sweetie is leaning back in his chair, calmly tapping his fingers together under his chin. He's so cool his mustache is starting to frost.

"An honest man is never nervous," Sweetie comments casually.

"A thief without an opportunity calls himself an honest man," Tax Man volleys back.

And the wife of the man who picks fights with the IRS gets conjugal visits.

"Do you need to see the W-2s?" Sweetie asks, pulling out a file.

"The eagle doesn't hunt flies," Tax Man huffs.

Taking his glasses out of their case, Tax Man carefully curls them behind his ears. Sighing, he starts combing through the financials.

"Whoa!" he says suddenly when he sees how much we pay in taxes. "This has gotta hurt!"

"I never begrudge paying taxes." Sweetie shrugs.

I turn to see if Sweetie is foaming at the mouth.

"The more you pay, the more money your business must be making," Sweetie explains. "Next year I hope we pay twice as much!"

Tax Man glances over the file at Sweetie. "It doesn't bother you that the average American works from January to May to pay his taxes?" he asks.

"Look at all we get for it," Sweetie says, squinting a bit as he sips his hot coffee.

"You're telling me it doesn't infuriate you to call the IRS for help, and even they can't figure it out?"

Sweetie blows it off with a flip of the hand. "That's why we pay our tax accountant out the nose."

"Come on," Tax Man says, leaning forward in his chair. "When we charge you twenty-one percent interest—PLUS penalties—doesn't it make you want to squeeze my 1099?!"

Sweetie leans across the desk to meet him. "It's a small price to pay for the freedom to own your own business and be your own boss."

Tax Man falls back in his chair. "You know what?" he suddenly asks, snapping his briefcase closed.

"Sweetie's future cellmate is a weight lifter named Roto-Rooter?" I whimper.

"No, you have termites." Slapping a tattered business card on Sweetie's desk, Tax Man heads for the door. "Give me a call."

"Sweetie," I say as we watch Tax Man drive away, "have you ever considered using your powers for good?"

"Too taxing," Sweetie says.

Paradise Lost

According to Sweetie, when it comes to sex there are three types of women—cats, buzzards, and pet rocks. Cats are picky, buzzards will land on anything, and a pet rock never has to be fed at all.

"We're going to start with some word associations," Dr. Dick says as he passes out the workbooks.

Thanks to a couple of friends of ours, Sweetie and I are at the Relationship Enrichment Seminar. So far, it's been about as informative as a refresher course on potty training.

It's pretty obvious whose idea it was to attend this thing. All the women are giddy at the prospect of spending four hours sitting in a semicircle discussing their emotional needs, while all the guys look like their Fruit of the Looms spent a little too much time in the dryer.

The only reason Sweetie hasn't bolted is the scenery. The woman sitting across from us has "buzzard" written all over her. She's dark, mysterious, and wearing a miniskirt that's one button away from being a figment of her imagination.

"Hallelujah!" Sweetie mutters every time she crosses her legs.

Dr. Dick drops a workbook on my desk and I barely have the cover broken in when Sweetie slams his closed and slaps his pencil on the top. Snatching it off his desk, I check his answers.

"The color you associate with your personality is polka dot?" I read skeptically. "And the body of water you associate with sexual intimacy is the condensation on an aluminum can?"

"I'm a complex guy." Sweetie shrugs. "Hallelujah!"

"Okay," Dr. Dick says, clapping his hands to signal we should finish our scribbling. "Who can tell me the key to relationship satisfaction."

"Emotional sharing and mutual respect," my girlfriend Angie calls out.

Dr. Dick pulls an air horn from behind the podium, points it at Angie, and blows. HONK!

"WRONG!" he shouts.

"Total honesty?" another woman calls out.

HONK! HONK! goes the horn.

"Common goals?" the woman beside me guesses.

HONK! HONK! HONK!

Turning his back to us, Dr. Dick scrapes a piece of chalk across the blackboard.

"The key to relationship satisfaction," he calls over his shoulder as he writes, "is SEXUAL COMPATIBILITY."

The guys light up like Christmas trees with Dr. Ruth angel ornaments on the top.

"If you have compatible sexual appetites," Dr. Dick explains clinically, "everyone in the relationship will be satisfied. If you don't, one of you will either go foraging in another field—or starve to death."

Frankly, a couple of these guys look like rigor mortis has already set in.

"Don't you think that's an oversimplification?" Angie frowns.

Dr. Dick rolls his eyes around the room at the guys. You could measure their beer bellies bouncing on the Richter scale.

"Next question," Dr. Dick says, propping his foot in the chair next to Ms. Miniskirt. "When I say *sexual intimacy*, what body of water comes to mind?"

Licking her lips in thought, Mini rubs her legs together like she's trying to start a fire. "The swimming pool at our country club," she finally says.

"And why is that?" Dr. Dick asks, leaning his elbow down on his knee.

"It's crystal clear," she says breathily.

"Hallelujah!" Sweetie mutters.

"And . . ." Dr. Dick motions for her to continue.

"You have to shower before you get in."

"Hallelujah!" Sweetie says, rolling his eyes toward heaven.

"And . . ." Dr. Dick says, leaning toward her.

"And the lanes are roped off so no one can bump into you."

Blinking, Sweetie looks like someone paved paradise and put up a parking lot. "Does that mean what I think it means?" Sweetie asks.

"In medical terms"—Dr. Dick sighs knowingly—"it's a classic case of a pet rock in buzzard's clothing."

Car Seats

You can tell what stage a relationship is in by the seats in a man's car.

When I first met Sweetie he had a Chevrolet with a bench seat the size of a Sealy Posturepedic. After we started going steady, he traded it for a Cutlass with bucket seats.

Now he has a truck. By the time a girl climbs over the stick shift, the emergency brake, the little thingy that shifts it into four-wheel drive, and the dual cup holder, she's forgotten why she made the trip.

It's just a matter of time before Sweetie is buckling me into a U-Haul.

"Sweetie," I yell across the King cab, "when did you start wearing glasses?"

"Around twenty years ago," he yells back.

That must have been about the time we got the Cutlass.

When it comes to relationships, you can never let your guard down. First it's bucket seats. Then it's separate TVs. While he's doing deep-breathing exercises to *Baywatch*, you're cleaning the screen with your tongue over David Duchovny on *The X-Files*.

The next thing you know, you're fighting over who gets custody of the cat. Of course, he doesn't really want the cat. He's just doing it out of spite. But try telling that to a cat-loving judge.

"Sweetie," I say, "we need to have a talk."

Sweetie shudders. Threatening Sweetie with "a talk" is like running a cattle prod up his inseam.

"Sweetie," I sigh, "we're drifting apart."

Reaching into the console, Sweetie pulls out a calendar. "Would you mind if we rescheduled this discussion for"—Sweetie counts on his fingers—"Tuesday?"

Sweetie watches my hormones like a farmer studies the *Farmer's Almanac.* He knows when to plow, when to plant, and when to give it a rest.

"Do you know how many of our friends from school are divorced?" I ask. "Every one of them!"

Sweetie freezes like a human mannequin. He figures if he doesn't breathe, I'll carry on both sides of the argument without him. Maybe that way he'll actually win one for a change.

"And do you know why all our friends are divorced?" I ask. "Because they all had bucket seats!"

Sweetie jots this one down in the notebook he keeps for the day he's going to have me committed.

"When was the last time we went parking?" I demand.

Sweetie lights a cigarette. If he'd known there was going to be a pop quiz on our way to the dump, he would have left the recyclables for another day.

"When we bought our first house!" I exclaim.

Signing on the dotted line for a thirty-year mortgage was like feeding Sweetie saltpeter. Every night for a month, we had to go parking in his mother's driveway. It didn't bother Sweetie's mom. She hadn't noticed he'd moved out.

"For the sake of our relationship," I sigh, ever the martyr, "I think we should go parking."

Taking a drag of his cigarette, Sweetie gives this some thought. "Could we drop off the garbage first?" he asks. "It's getting a little ripe."

"And we need to stop by the store."

After twenty years together, Sweetie and I may not respond like rack-and-pinion steering, but when it comes to overall performance, we take a backseat to no one.

With Friends Like These, Who Needs Drugs?

Doctor, Doctor, Give Me a Call

My girlfriend is torn between two lovers. One is a doctor, and the other, an unemployed motorcycle mechanic who's currently living in the backseat of his car. Normally, I'm not one to jump to conclusions, but in this particular instance, I'm already in free fall.

"What kind of car?" I ask.

"Peugeot," Kat says.

This pretty much confirms my theory that bachelor number two is going nowhere.

Still, a relationship is more than the sum of its parts. It would have to be. You couldn't buy a cup of coffee with what you'd get for a used Peugeot at a chop shop.

"So which one do you have the most in common with?" I ask, studying the menu.

"The doctor," Kat says, twirling her hair in thought.

"Which one is the easier to talk to?"

"The doctor," she says, chewing on a cuticle.

"And which one is the better . . . pianist?"

"The doctor," she says, without hesitation.

Eyebrows raised, I glance up from my menu. I just naturally assumed that a man who could tune a Harley would be much better with his hands than your average surgeon.

"So the doctor is more intelligent, more ambitious, and better in the hay?"

Kat shrugs sheepishly.

"Why are we having this conversation?"

It has been my experience that in every situation, there is always one right choice. And inevitably, Kat turns left. When it comes to mating, some women are like salmon—they just keep swimming up the same creek.

"It's just that Harley is"—Kat shivers—"so-oooh good-looking."

Granted, I have about as much depth as a Dixie Cup, but sometimes my friends are so shallow, even I'm appalled.

"Looks fade," I say, "but a doctor will always retain his re-sale value."

Kat slides an $8\frac{1}{2}$-by-11 glossy of Harley across the table.

If I were a man, I'd have to cross my legs.

Prying my fingers off the photo, Kat does her best to smooth the creases out. Between the slobber and the gnawed corner, poor Harley looks like he's been rode hard and put up wrinkled.

"Sorry," I mutter.

"No problem," she says. "I keep the original at home."

On this note, I pause for a moment of silent reflection. There's nothing I hate more than having my convictions put to the test. That's why I try not to have any.

"Kat," I sigh, "behind door number one is financial security, emotional fulfillment, and intellectual equity. Behind door number two is a four-ounce spray bottle of piña colada car freshener. Which door will it be?"

Frowning, Kat bites her lip gloss.

Obviously, we're going to have to take this to a higher authority.

"The universe gives each of us our own unique gifts," the waitress says, holding Harley's mangled photo at arm's length.

Kat and I nod solemnly.

"On the one hand, the doctor is blessed with brains and

bucks. On the other hand, Harley is built like Hoover Dam and fills out a pair of jeans like the creme filling in a Hostess Twinkie."

Taking a deep soulful breath, the waitress stares off toward the all-you-can-eat salad bar. "I ask you, what kind of human beings would we be to say one is superior to the other?"

Kat rolls her eyes at me, and I hang my head in snobbish shame.

"Follow your bliss!" the waitress declares. "Choose Harley!"

"It works for me," Kat says, falling back against her chair.

"All right, all right," I grumble. "I'll dance at your wedding . . . again."

"Now that we've taken care of that," the waitress says, flipping open her pad and pulling a pencil from behind her ear, "what's the number of that doctor?"

The Mortician

"Four . . . five . . . six . . ." Leila counts under her breath.

To pass the time while we wait in line to view the casket, Leila is counting face-lifts. There's nothing like a funeral to make you contemplate the brevity of life—or the importance of good skin care.

"Considering what they charge for funerals," I say, squinting to read the card on a wreath of chrysanthemums, "you'd think they could afford a sixty-watt bulb."

"Then again," Leila says, turning her face from side to side to check her reflection on a brass urn, "a girl never looks better than in indirect lighting."

Indirect lighting or not, Leila looks great. Across the room, three pallbearers are checking her out like they're just dying to lay her to rest.

When it comes to fashion, I can have them panting down at the recycle center, but I've never quite mastered funeral chic. Leila, on the other hand, should have been a mortician.

"Mourning becomes you, Leila," I say.

"I know," she says. "I was born to wear shrouds."

The line moves, and Leila and I step forward.

"How does my skin look?" she asks, turning her face up for my inspection.

"Good." I shrug automatically. Then I do a double take. Actually, it is looking better than usual.

"Preparation H," she whispers in my ear.

"You mean . . . on your face?!"

"It gives prompt, temporary relief to puffiness," Leila says, pointing to her bagless eyes like Vanna White, "and shrinks swollen pores."

"Cream or ointment?" I demand, grabbing her by her double-breasted black lapels.

I have no idea what the long-term side effects of smearing hemorrhoid medication on your face are, but my mouth is already starting to pucker.

"Soft as a baby's behind," Leila adds, tilting her cheek for me to feel.

It's just a matter of time before Leila and I start bathing in formaldehyde.

The line moves forward again, and I find myself standing side by side with a pink Princess phone, the receiver dangling off the hook.

"Don't hang it up!" Leila cries, blocking me like Wilt Chamberlain.

"What?!" I gasp, jumping back and dropping the receiver like it bit me.

"It's a representational flower arrangement," Leila explains as the pink receiver swings back and forth. "It signifies that she's been 'called home.' "

Actually, I'd prefer they send a fax. I'm starting to get this little crease from holding the phone with my chin.

Heads tilted and hands clasped, Leila and I finally stare down at the deceased.

"Ninety-seven is much younger than it used to be," Leila sighs.

"And getting younger all the time," I say.

"She looks good," Leila says.

"Very natural." I nod.

"Her skin tone is flawless," Leila says, moving closer.

"Poreless as porcelain," I say, moving in right beside her.

"And there isn't a wrinkle on her face," Leila says incredulously.

Raising onto our toes, we lean over the casket.

"Hell, she didn't look this good when she was alive!" Leila says.

You could frost mugs in the basement of Fennel's Funeral Home. Blowing on my hands, I stomp my feet to get the feeling back in my toes.

"So it's your theory," Leila says, talking a little shop with Mr. Fennel as he works on a *client*, "that if fifty-six degrees slows rigor mortis, it's bound to prevent wrinkles?"

"Leila," I mumble, teeth chattering, "you've lost your mind."

Looking at me over his Coke-bottle glasses, Mr. Fennel inspects me like a bug. "I give you two years"—he smirks—"and you'll be begging me for a mortician makeover."

The Mighty Emu

"I've been thinking about emus," Charlie says.

"Emus." I nod. "Aren't they like big chickens?"

Charlie and I used to work together. Every couple of months or so he swings through town and buys my lunch, compliments of his company credit card.

"Emus are really up and coming," Charlie says, checking for red as he slices into the slab of prime rib flopped across his plate.

"They sell emu futures?" I ask, buttering a roll.

"Nope," he says, pointing his fork at me. "I'm going to quit my job and grow them."

From engineer to chicken farmer . . . movin' on up!

There comes a time in everyone's life when you wake up and say to yourself, "This isn't a job—it's hell with a benefit package."

"Charlie," I say, crunching on a cucumber, "have you ever seen an emu?"

Once you've made the decision to move on, you instantly develop the short-timer's attitude. With a smirk on your face, you glance around at your coworkers and think, Looo-sers.

"Wasn't that an emu in *Green Eggs and Ham?*" I ask.

You're charged with the exhilaration of change. Your possibilities are limitless, but you're not fussy. As long as there's international travel, a company credit card, and unlimited golf involved, you could be happy.

"They're very docile," Charlie says as he whips out a brochure:

Emus—Your Path to Financial Independence

You're a humble person by nature, but a prestigious title would be nice—perhaps something like "Chancellor of the Exchequer."

"Definitely docile," I say, staring into the beady eyes of an $8^1/_2$-by-11 full-color glossy emu.

You call up the guy at the employment agency and inform him that this is his lucky day. You've decided to change careers—something different, new, exciting—maybe something that would benefit mankind. There's a long pause on the phone . . . followed by a dial tone.

"Charlie," I say, "do they allow emus at your condo?"

You pick up the Sunday paper, comb through the want ads, and come to the rather stark realization that if you were to leave your current position, you might actually have to *work* for a living.

"Fillet emu," I say.

"It could happen," Charlie says.

You network all your networks, contact all your contacts, and work all your coworkers, and are dismayed to discover they're hoping you're calling to offer *them* a better job.

"Wow, I had no idea an emu could run forty miles per hour," I say, reading the brochure.

You dust off your résumé and it disintegrates in your hands.

". . . And they produce five pounds of manure per day— *each*."

You begin to have the nagging suspicion that you're not really qualified to do anything. In fact, you're pretty sure you couldn't get the job you've got now.

"Charlie," I say, "how many emus do you suppose it's going to take to make a mortgage payment and two car payments and put three kids through college?"

"I can't take it anymore," Charlie whimpers.

"I know," I say, patting his hand. "But, honey, the only thing you know how to grow is hair."

And frankly, my little emu, that's not thriving like it used to.

Bucket and the Duck

I'm propped on top of a toolbox at my mechanic's garage. I've spent many an afternoon keeping this spot warm. I've never been much for those quickie joints. Call me old-fashioned, but I like a man who knows his way around my chassis and is familiar with my timing.

"What happened to your tailgate?" Joe asks, handing me a Coke in the little bottle.

"A tree ran into it," I say, wiping the mouth of the bottle off with my T-shirt.

"Those trees never look where they're going," Joe says, digging bark out of the bumper with a screwdriver.

Joe has a body-shop manner that won't quit. Just another reason why, when it comes to mechanics, I'm strictly monogamous. I haven't let another man gap my plugs since college.

The phone rings and Joe jogs off to his office to answer it. Dipping a little lanolin hand cleaner out of the pot, I align myself with the shop fan and settle back to Patsy Cline on the radio.

A good garage is like a poor girl's country club. The sodas are icy, the Snickers are fresh, and the guys have arms that are steel belted. Forget Nautilus. Nothing builds muscle like pumping Michelins.

Suddenly, through the glass window, Joe jerks the phone

receiver to arm's length, mouths a few four-letter words, then slams it down into the cradle with a crash.

"I told him not to marry her," Bucket mumbles. Pulling a cherry Tootsie Roll Pop out of his mouth, he yells down into the grease pit, "Didn't I tell him not to marry that girl?"

"You told him, Bucket," Duck yells from under my truck.

Without looking, Bucket reaches into a toolbox, pulls out a socket wrench, and stretches his arm down into the pit. "I said to him, 'Sure she's good-lookin', but that woman's crazy.' "

Taking the wrench, Duck nods. "That woman's crazy."

"But once your engine starts revvin'," Bucket clucks, "the flag is down."

The phone rings again, and Joe just stares at it.

"She must call here thirty times a day," Bucket huffs, pulling an oil filter off the shelf, taking it out of the box, then passing it down into the pit.

"At least thirty," Duck says as he inspects the filter, then disappears under my truck.

There's a clunk as the nut falls into the pan, followed by the sound of old oil spilling into the funnel.

"Of course," Bucket says solemnly, "my wife's crazy, too."

Leaning against the wall of the pit, Duck lights a cigarette and waits for the oil to finish draining. "I told you not to marry her," he says on the exhale. "Didn't I tell you not to marry her?"

Sniffing, Bucket rolls the Tootsie Pop from one side of his mouth to the other.

"You know," Bucket says slowly, "I'm startin' to think maybe all women are crazy."

Grunting, Duck flicks his cigarette butt out the garage door, then ducks back under my truck.

"How long you been married, Bucket?" I ask.

Rolling his eyes up to the ceiling, Bucket does a little

math. "All together . . . I'd say around twelve years. But this one's only had her hooks into me the last couple."

"How many times have you been married?"

"Four," he says, "if you don't count that time in Vegas."

Staring at my old oil filter, Duck swings out from under my truck and slams right into my dented bumper. Grimacing, he touches his forehead, then checks his fingers for blood.

"Vegas," Bucket sighs, tossing Duck a clean shop cloth. "Boy, was *that* one crazy!"

They say the definition of insanity is doing the same thing over and over while expecting a different result. But having backed into the same tree three times, I'm probably not the person to point this out.

It's My Monkey

Emmy has her leg sticking out of her Volvo even before it skids to a stop in Leila's driveway. Running into the kitchen, she jerks open a kitchen drawer and rummages around until she finds her stash. Tearing open the Ziploc bag, she rips a Virginia Slim out of the pack with her teeth and flicks her Bic.

"Ahhhh," she sighs, falling against the counter.

"I take it your husband still thinks you've quit," I say, taking a sip of coffee.

"I like to think of it as a drill," Emmy says as she rubs tobacco on her gums, "for that time when they finally outlaw cigarettes."

"Doesn't he wonder why you dash out of the house a dozen times a day?" Rosie frowns.

"He thinks I'm having an affair with Leila," Emmy says, blowing smoke into the stove exhaust, "but otherwise, everything's hunky-dory."

Some women find men's obsession with sex annoying. But for those of us who know how to use it, it's as handy as an elastic waistband.

"Coffee?" Leila asks Emmy as she refills our cups.

"Can't," Emmy says, taking one last drag, then throwing the incriminating evidence down the garbage disposal. "We have dinner guests. They think I'm in the kitchen getting the appetizers."

Spritzing with Fresh Breath, Emmy is halfway out the door when she suddenly stops dead in her tracks. "Can I borrow some dip?"

Sitting around Leila's kitchen table, Leila, Rosie, and I watch Emmy burn rubber down the drive. It's only a matter of time before the surgeon general requires smokers in nicotine withdrawal to wear a warning label.

"I never kept any secrets from my husband," Rosie says, twirling the string around her herbal tea bag to squeeze it dry.

"Did he keep any from you?" Leila asks, her chin resting on her hand.

"Other than the twenty-four-year-old dental hygienist he ran off with, I don't think so."

In a perfect world, guys who run off with twenty-four-year-olds would have a much higher mortality rate than a four-pack-a-day man.

"Personally, I think smoking should be against the law," Rosie says.

Slowly stirring her tea, she tings the spoon dry against the side of her cup. "And I really think we should take a look at coffee. It causes nervousness and is addictive. Coffee used to be illegal, you know."

Rosie has no faults. As soon as we kill her, we're going to have her canonized.

"Rosie," I say as I try to steady my hand enough to pour another cup of coffee, "mess with my drug, and I'll hurt you."

About this time, Emmy's Volvo cuts across the lawn and screeches to a stop in the driveway.

"That was quick," Leila says as Emmy slides to a stop on the kitchen linoleum.

"Not quick enough," Emmy says, taking a hit off her cigarette. "Nothing I hate more than being around a holier-than-thou nonsmoker."

On that note, Rosie stares at her tea like she's reading her future.

"You can smell the Ring Dings on the wife's breath," Emmy says, bending over the counter and snorting a few fallen ashes, ". . . and she's lecturing *me* on health and social responsibility?"

"I wasn't aware that secondhand Ring Dings were hazardous to your health," Rosie says, "but no doubt it needs to be studied."

"Time for salad," Emmy grumbles as she buries her cigarette butt in the cat's litter box.

"Bon appétit," Leila calls as Emmy flies out the door.

"What does Emmy do when they're on vacation?" Rosie asks as we watch Emmy's Volvo sideswipe the garbage can.

"Wears a nicotine patch under her bikini," Leila says.

"Doesn't her husband wonder about that?" Rosie asks.

"He thinks it's hormones," Leila says. "Last year she faked a hysterectomy."

At the Movies

According to Sweetie, if two couples were meant to couple, there'd be a word for it.

"Don't you just hate people who talk in movies," Rita says, nose wrinkled.

"Nothing irritates me more!" I say.

Sweetie and I are at the movies with Rita and Roger, a couple we recently hit it off with at a party.

"Hope you don't mind," Roger says, "but we prefer sitting close to the screen."

Sweetie and I glance at each other. It's a match *Made in Heaven*.

Scooping up their snacks, Rita and Roger follow Sweetie and me to our usual spot, second row, dead center. Sweetie and I have spent so much time in these seats, they've perfectly contoured to fit our bodies and automatically fold down when they see us coming.

"That new film with that actress who was in that movie that was directed by the guy who was in that TV show about the bigot looks good," Roger says as we watch the movie facts.

"Meg Ryan, *Sleepless in Seattle*, Rob Reiner, *All in the Family*," Rita translates, grabbing a handful of popcorn.

"I didn't know she had a new film out," I say, tearing the cellophane off the Raisinets with my teeth.

"Uh-huh," Roger mumbles, mouth full of Gummi Bears.

"Who's the male lead?" Sweetie asks, measuring popcorn in his palm to achieve the precise Raisinet-to-popcorn ratio.

"Honey," Roger suddenly says to Rita, "does the screen look out of focus to you?"

"Looks out of focus to me, sweetheart," Rita says, squinting up at the screen.

Handing Rita his Coke, Roger stands up and turns toward the projection room.

"FOCUS THE SCREEN!" he bellows.

Simultaneously, Sweetie and I have a stroke.

"Oh, you know," Roger continues, dropping back into his seat, "that guy who was in that movie with the guy who used to be really great but got fat, and there were all those wild animals."

"Ooooh . . . it's right on the tip of my tongue!" Rita says, snapping her fingers.

"Excuse me," the woman sitting behind us says as she sticks her head between Rita and Roger. "Are you referring to the man who's married to the woman with the incredible body, who was in that movie with the Flying Elvises?"

"Right!" Roger says.

"Matthew Broderick," the woman says, very pleased with herself.

Smiling at Roger, she gets him in an eye lock and pins him down for a solid three seconds before dropping back onto her seat.

The heat radiating off Rita's face could melt nacho cheese dip. Meanwhile, Roger innocently smacks away at his Gummi Bears.

"Lucky guess," Rita mumbles.

"Hardly," the woman huffs back.

"You really have to be desperate to eavesdrop at a theater," Rita spits over her shoulder.

The woman kicks the back of Rita's seat.

And the next thing we know, Rita is climbing over the seat and snacks are flying like an Oklahoma bake sale in *Twister*.

In the midst of the clawing, hair pulling, and shrieks going on behind us, Roger stands up and hollers, "WILL SOME-BODY FOCUS THE SCREEN?!"

Frozen, Sweetie and I stare at the fascinating movie facts.

"Gee," Sweetie says as Rita's shoe goes sailing by, "I always wondered what the grip did."

A flying knee hits Roger in the back of the head, and he sprays Gummi Bears across the theater like a semiautomatic. Splattering onto the screen, they stick like Superglue.

"Honey!" Roger calls over his shoulder as the lights dim. "Movie's starting!"

Hiking up her skirt, Rita crawls back into our row and settles into her seat.

"Do you suppose someone should peel the Gummi Bears off?" I whisper.

"SSSSSSHHHH!" Roger and Rita hiss simultaneously.

RIF

When Bob told Beth he was getting RIF-ed, she thought he was going to the spa for a colonic cleansing. As anyone who's been there knows, she wasn't that far off.

"You've been fired?" Beth frowns as she rereads Bob's pink slip.

"Not fired," Bob says, plucking a club cozy off his three-wood. "I'm part of a 'reduction in force.'"

"Reduction in force," Beth repeats slowly. "Couldn't you just promise to be more gentle?"

We're sitting in Bob's study, which is located in the left wing of Beth and Bob's home, which is roughly the size of Denmark. While Sweetie pours over their finances, Beth refills our coffee from her silver service and Bob cleans his golf clubs with a chamois.

"Well," Bob says, steaming his Ping putter with his breath and buffing it to a mirror shine, "how bad is it?"

"I project you can continue at your current standard of living, for about"—Sweetie hits the total on his calculator—"one hour and fifteen minutes, providing there are no unexpected expenditures."

"What about with my severance pay?" Bob asks as he studies his grip.

"One hour and twenty minutes," Sweetie says dryly.

Bob will never have old money. He seems to be under the impression it comes with an expiration date, and it's better to burn it than to let it compound.

"So we trim a little fat." Bob shrugs as he drops a Titleist golf ball onto the Oriental rug. "Honey, start a list."

Beth runs to her armoire for her monogrammed notepad with matching pen.

"Number one," Beth says as she writes, "cancel the coffee club."

"That's my girl," Bob says, taking a few practice swings.

"For richer, for poorer, my darling," she says adoringly.

Maintaining a firm grip, Bob blows her a kiss.

"Number two, cancel the pool service."

"I did it before," Bob says, chipping the ball into the wet-bar sink. "I can do it again."

". . . lawn service, laundry service, maid service . . ."

"Darling, this is the best thing that's ever happened to us," Bob declares, dropping another ball on the rug. "We'll feel like newlyweds again!"

". . . manicures, pedicures, facials, massages . . ."

"Who says Americans can't tighten the belt when the need arises!" Bob declares, sailing a ball down the marble foyer.

"Public school system, here we come!" Beth sings, her pen flying like Bernstein's baton over the New York Philharmonic.

"If it was good enough for Reagan," Bob roars as his ball ricochets off the skylight, "it's good enough for Bobby, Jr.!"

". . . country club membership, *au revoir!*" Beth chirps.

Bob freezes on the upswing as if the video replay tape broke. "The club?" he gasps, turning frantically to Sweetie.

In debt do they part.

"FORE!" Sweetie nods.

"But I get unemployment, right?" Bob insists. "I mean, I've paid taxes for twenty-five years. If anyone deserves to get something back, you're looking at him, right?"

"Bob, your unemployment check is going to be even lower than your IQ."

Bob stares at Sweetie like a deer caught in golf-cart headlights.

Slipping the putter out of his limp hand, Beth slaps a Post-it on Bob's golf bag that reads: YARD SALE.

"I hate to leave them like this," Sweetie says as we walk to our car.

"Don't worry about it," I say as I wave good-bye. "Beth has a coffee can in the closet that could pay off the national debt."

Babysitting

The other day Mindy called and asked me to babysit her kid.

"You mean in *this* lifetime?" I ask. "I don't think so."

"Grow some estrogen!" she snaps.

Don't get me wrong. There's nothing cuter than a little boy. I just happen to believe they fall into that category of "animals that cannot be domesticated and belong in the wild."

A herd of renegade elephants on a rampage couldn't do the damage Mindy's kid can do, left unattended in my living room. This kid tried to drown my fish.

And Dad is no help at all. The minute Kid's potty-trained, Dad crams a little helmet on his head, plants a football in his tiny little gut, and screams, "Go tackle something!" By the time Kid reaches his teens, there isn't an inch of his little body that hasn't been scraped, burned, cut, or nearly knocked off.

Then he turns sixteen, and just as Mom is sighing a breath of relief, Dad throws him the keys to the car—two tons of metal and glass searing down the highway at the speed of light. If you treated a dog like this, you'd get arrested. I'm telling you, someone needs to start a humane society for boys.

"Everything you need to know is here," Mindy speed-talks as she shoves a laminated "Babysitter's Guide" into my hand.

"Where is he?" I ask.

Mindy's eyes roll to the ceiling, where the faint but steady tap of computer keys can be heard.

"He's playing with his new computer game that his dad got him," Mindy says. "Tortures of the Spanish Inquisition."

I close my eyes and groan.

"Get a grip!" she calls back over her shoulder as she flies out the door.

Mindy runs across the lawn as fast as her legs will carry her. As her car burns rubber down the drive, I am suddenly struck with the distinct possibility that she's never coming back. You can bet I wouldn't.

Under the circumstances, I think it's wise to review my "Babysitter's Guide." As I do with most instructional material, I quickly fade into staring at a grease spot behind the stove that looks just like Roseanne.

"What are you doing?" Mindy's kid asks, catching me completely off guard.

"Staring," I say.

"At what?"

"Nothing." I shrug. I'm not about to admit that I'm fixating on a bacon blot.

Mindy's kid and I size each other up. He's about four feet tall, weighs maybe fifty pounds soaking wet, and has a face that could be on a Christmas card. I'm doomed.

"How are your fish?" he asks.

"Afraid of water, thank you."

It's becoming apparent that Mindy's kid is sliding suspiciously toward the fridge as he talks. His baby-blue eyes still fixed on me, he slowly opens the door and takes out a Coke.

While I am not naturally endowed with the maternal instinct, I sense something is rotten in Denmark, so I check my "Babysitter's Guide."

"You're not allowed to have Coke," I say as I scan the Thou-shalt-nots. "It makes you hyper."

Kid glares at me, so I glare back. I can hear the gears grinding in his devious little head.

"My mom says you cut your hair with a Weed Eater."

What can I tell you; the kid's good.

"Would you like ice with that?" I say, popping the top for him.

It seems to me that dealing with little boys is a lot like playing poker. You need to know when to hold them, when to fold them, and when to walk away. But the most important thing you need to know is, oral contraceptives are only 97 percent effective.

Sweetie in Babeland

Sweetie used to love women. I could throw him into a room full of females and he was like a babe in Toyland. Nowadays, leaving a girlfriend alone with him is like dropping her off at a roach motel.

"Sweetie!" Rachel cries, throwing her arms out for a hug.

Sweetie slams to a stop like a mime hitting an imaginary wall. Waving sheepishly, he moonwalks back into the house.

"Was it something I said?" Rachel frowns, arms still hanging in the air.

"Why didn't you just pull the welcome mat out from under her?" I hiss as I slam the coffee tray on the kitchen counter.

Sweetie grunts from behind *The Wall Street Journal*.

"I don't get it," I say. "When we were in college, you loved my girlfriends."

"Bring a couple of college girls home," Sweetie's little brother, Rolex, says as he inventories the goodies in the refrigerator, "and watch our transformation."

"Childbearing takes a lot out of a woman," I defend as I look through the window at Rachel chatting with the yard art.

"And motherhood sucks the rest out like a Hoover," Rolex adds, staring over my shoulder.

"Tell that to Goldie Hawn," Sweetie says absently from behind the paper. "Over fifty years old with a litter of kids, and she could still go-go-dance in a cage."

"Not all women aspire to be hamsters," I say as I watch Rachel pick sunflower seeds out of the bird feeder and stuff them in her cheek.

"It's a shame," Sweetie sighs. "Rachel was never that bright, but she was a real cutie."

"Another one bites the dust," Rolex says as he cracks open a bowl of leftovers and sniffs.

"Who'd have ever guessed she'd turn into an H.M.O.," Sweetie sighs, shaking his head.

"And H.M.O. would be Male Moron Code for . . ."

"Hypochondriac mother who's overweight," Rolex explains, checking a glass for water spots.

"I'll bet you ten bucks the only thing Rachel talks about is her health, her kids, and her weight," Sweetie says.

"You can't judge a woman just by her cover," I insist, arms crossed.

"With our eyes closed," Rolex says, throwing a ten-dollar bill on the counter.

"So, Rachel," Sweetie chats as Rolex refills her coffee cup, "what have you been up to?"

"Well . . ."

Two hours later.

". . . So after my hysterectomy I tried the patch, but it gave me a rash. Not your typical rash. You know how most rashes are red with those little bumps? This rash was like smallpox. I looked like someone dipped me in honey and tied me to a beehive."

Rachel pauses long enough to cram a wedge of Brie in her mouth.

". . . I'm using the cream now, but I think it's reacting with one of the other six"—Rachel counts on her fingers—". . . seven medications I'm on. That's why I can't lose the baby fat."

Rachel takes a sip of coffee. "Did I mention my third child was a breech?" she asks, looking up over her cup.

"Yes," Rolex says, feet kicked up and hands behind his head, "but do tell us again."

"I don't take checks," Sweetie whispers in my ear as I follow Rachel to her car.

"It's a real shame about Sweetie," Rachel sighs as she digs in her purse for her car keys. "I had the worst crush on him when we were in school. Who'd have guessed he'd turn into a G.O.P."

"G.O.P.?" I frown.

"Grumpy old phart."

If I Had a Woman Like That

After they stripped the old shingles off the house and dumped them on top of her rhododendrons, Rosie's roofers left to get a little lunch. We haven't seen them since.

"Did you give them any money?" Leila asks as we watch the gutter swing back and forth on one nail, then fall off the house.

Two things a woman should never do if she wants a man to fix something around the house—pay him or marry him.

"It's going to rain, isn't it?" Rosie says, looking up at the dark sky.

"For forty days and forty nights," Maxine assures her.

"Will that hurt anything?" Rosie frowns.

Leila, Max, and I roll eyes at each other. If Rosie were a chick, she'd still be in the shell.

"Your decking will warp, your insulation will rot, and your heating bills will bankrupt you," Max says knowingly. "Then your ceiling will collapse and your hardwood floors will buckle like the Grand Tetons."

"This sort of thing never happens to Martha Stewart," Rosie sighs as she bends down to prop up a stomped hosta, using a gutter spike as a splint.

Besides shingles, Rosie's lawn is littered with cans, cigarette butts, and Hostess Twinkie wrappers. If there were a couple of Porta Potties, it'd look just like Woodstock.

Suddenly Rosie bolts to a stand. "Do you know why workmen never do this to Martha Stewart?"

Leila looks up from her coffee. "Because she'd cut off their maracas, dip them in glitter, and hang them on her Christmas tree?"

"Because she feeds them!" Rosie declares.

Huddled at Rosie's kitchen window, Leila, Max, and I watch the roofers pile out of the truck.

"Is that man wearing prison pants?" Leila whispers.

"Actually," I say, "his gold tooth and the handcuffs dangling off his belt pull the ensemble together quite nicely."

In the midst of all this stands Rosie at a garden brunch buffet that would make Martha proud.

"I thought you gentlemen might like a bite to eat before work," Rosie says, pouring them each a little glass of fresh-squeezed orange juice.

"Thank goodness we talked her out of the place cards," Max whispers.

Glancing at each other, the roofers seem to come to a silent consensus. Awkwardly, they take seats and stuff pink cloth napkins into their collars.

"What is that?" Tater asks, pointing to the eggs Benedict.

"Hollandaise sauce," Rosie says. "I like to add a touch of nutmeg."

Taking out his pocketknife, Tater scrapes the sauce off and slings it onto the empty milk carton he just threw in the yard.

"Well," Rosie says, backing away from the patio, "bon appétit!"

"Now that's a lady," Bo says, leaning sideways to watch Rosie round the corner. "Wonder what happened to her husband?"

Preacher sniffs the mango chutney. "My guess is she starved him to death."

Salting his entire plate, Tater cautiously takes a bite. Midchew, he cracks open his mouth and picks something off his tongue.

"What is that?" he asks, holding his finger out.

Bo leans over, tilts his head sideways, and studies it. "Looks like a pimiento."

Flick, and the pimiento splats in for a landing on top of the hollandaise sauce.

"Yes, sir," Bo says, putting his hands behind his head and kicking his feet up on Rosie's trellis, "if I had me a woman like that, I'd be the kind of man who'd have me a house like this."

"The fish don't bait the hook, boy," Preacher says, sniffing the hazelnut coffee.

Suddenly Tater spits something across the yard, then furiously scrubs his tongue with Rosie's ironed and Downy-fresh napkin.

"This fish would have to come with a burger and fries before I'd reel her in!"

The Artist

In my family, anything with Elvis on it was considered art. If the hips moved, Dad had it insured.

"Are you a sculptor?" the guy standing next to me at the refreshment table asks.

"Why?" I ask as I chop off a piece of white chocolate and pop it into my mouth.

"Because you're eating the marble cutting board," he says.

You know you're out of your element when you eat the serving utensils.

It's opening night at a friend's art exhibit. The gallery is packed with artsy types waxing eloquent about art while balancing wineglasses and little plates of fruit and cheese. I don't know flip about art, but I can balance food with the best of them.

"When I work," the guy says, picking up a grape and studying it, "I eat my paint."

He sticks out his tongue and it's covered with streaks of red and black. Apparently, oil paint isn't fattening. I could pick this boy up and use him as an eyeliner brush.

"Have you tried the Brie?" I garble, with a mouth full of marble.

After a simply fascinating discussion on the difference in flavor between oil and acrylic, I leave Bristle Boy and wander over to where Sweetie, Charlie, and Charlie's fiancée, Twinkie, are standing in front of a sculpture of a woman.

"It's called *Torso of a Woman*," Sweetie reads off the program.

"How much?" Charlie asks.

Tilting the program, Sweetie points at the price.

"Nah," Charlie says, moving on to the next piece. "I can get a year of *Playboy* for eight hundred bucks less—and those nudies have heads."

It's comforting to know that no matter how rich you are, you can still be dumb as a rock.

Meandering from piece to piece, Charlie suddenly slams to a stop in front of a huge bundle of twisted and shredded steel cable shaped like a headless man running.

"It's called *Flight of American Industry*," Sweetie reads.

Eyes narrowed in concentration, Sweetie, Charlie, Twinkie, and I study it. While I can appreciate the power of the piece and the intricacy of the craftsmanship, it looks like a scarecrow to me.

"What do you think, Twink?" Charlie asks.

"Whatever you think, baby," Twinkie says.

"I think I want it!" Charlie announces. "It'll look great in the john."

Every aloft head in the lofty room turns to stare at us.

"He also shows movies in the bathroom," Sweetie says to the gaping crowd. "He calls it the *Can Film Festival*."

"How much?" Charlie demands as he lovingly strokes the scarecrow.

Tilting the program, Sweetie points to the five-digit number.

"Small price to pay for art!" Charlie declares, grabbing Twinkie's arm and storming off toward the gallery owner.

Taking his own sweet time, Sweetie strolls off after Charlie, singing, ". . . if he only had a brain."

For some reason, I find myself drawn again to the *Torso of a Woman*. I can't explain it, but I can't stop looking at it. When I finally come up for air, I notice there's a man standing next to me. This guy is a *real* artist.

Taking a long draw on his cigarette, the artist studies the curves of the sculpture. Slowly his face begins to soften and his eyes grow moist.

"It's really good, isn't it?" I say.

"Art is neither good nor bad," the artist says. "It can only reflect the person who's looking at it."

Sighing, he reaches out his callused fingers to touch the stone. "The best we can hope for is that, maybe, if we're lucky, something we create will lift one person beyond what they are."

"Hey!" Charlie yells at me from across the room. "Should I get the headless chick for the guest bath?"

"You might lift some of the people some of the time," I tell the artist, "but some of them really need to be flushed."

Butt . . .

"What is she thinking?" Leila mutters as we watch Maxine come bouncing out of the dressing room in a full-body zip-up black-lace unitard.

Cher can pull it off, but stuff your average woman into a black unitard, and we look like charred bratwurst.

With the guys glued to the sports network down at Radio Shack, Leila, Maxine, and I are shopping till we drop at the Moonlight Madness Sale. Moonlight Madness is when a woman starts thinking that as the percent off gets bigger, her hips get smaller.

Under these conditions, a woman is likely to do anything. I once bought a fire-engine-red Donna Karan thong bikini. From the rear I looked like a Little Caesar's ad—Pizza Pizza.

Taking a slow turn at the four-way mirror, Maxine suddenly opens her eyes to the size of a satellite dish and lets out a bloodcurdling scream.

Head stretched back over her shoulder, she spins around and around like a dog chasing its tail, then collapses on the floor in a heap. Her plump lacy legs sprawled out in front of her, Max stares straight ahead in a glassy-eyed stupor.

"Get back! Make way!" I say, pushing through the gawking women with price tags hanging all over them.

The path cleared, Leila rushes to Maxine's side.

"Is she a doctor?" a woman with a Miracle Bra on the outside of her T-shirt asks.

"No," I say, "but she's married to one."

Awestruck, a murmur filters through the crowd.

Calling upon all her medical expertise, Leila takes Maxine's hand and pats it. "Max, Max, talk to us, honey."

When her lips finally start to move, Leila leans down and puts her ear up to Max's mouth. Finally, taking a deep breath, Leila stands up.

"It's a severe case of *clunis delabor*," Leila says solemnly. "Butt drop."

Gasping, the crowd shrinks back in horror.

"It isn't contagious, for Gucci's sake!" Leila snaps as she loosens Maxine's mock-lace turtleneck and props her up against the mirror.

"How bad is it?" I ask, glancing over Leila's shoulder.

"Critical," Leila says, which is the medical term for "submarines can't sink this low."

Instinctively, every woman in the place does ten quick tushy tucks.

It is one of life's cruel little jokes that you're sailing along thinking everything's shipshape, when suddenly one day you glance back over your shoulder and your stern is dragging bottom like a trawler.

Leila and I have just about coaxed Maxine to a stand when Harold, her husband, wanders up wanting Coke money. He gets one look at Max in the four-way and freaks.

"Aaaagh!" he screams, throwing his hands over his face.

War may be hell, but nothing tests a man's character like seeing his wife in a see-through unitard under fluorescent lighting.

While I grab him by the shoulders, Leila shoves his head into a Victoria's Secret bag and holds it there until he stops hyperventilating.

"Now, when she's feeling strong enough," Leila says as she

jots the prescription down, "I want you to take her over to lingerie and have her fitted with a girdle."

We glance down at Max's former tight end. Unless that girdle has FORKLIFT painted across the side, we all know this is an exercise in futility.

"Then, first thing Monday morning, I want to see her in a step class."

Leila rips the sheet of paper off the tablet and hands it to Harold.

"W-w-will it ever be . . . like it was?" Harold asks, voice cracking.

"With our love and support," Leila says, patting him on his slumped shoulders, "it'll be up and round in no time."

Wiping a little drool from the corner of Maxine's slack mouth, Harold gently leads her away.

"What are her odds?" I ask as we watch them fade into Accessories.

"They'll raise the *Titanic* before that tub floats to sea level again."

Maxine's Diet

"You gonna eat that, or not?" Maxine snaps.

Before I have time to answer, she snatches the olive off my plate, sucks the pimiento out, and tosses the gutless remains on a pile on her plate.

"I was saving that," I say.

"You want it back?" Max growls.

Max is in the "rabid dog" stage of dieting. Her brain has deteriorated and she's foaming at the mouth. Any minute, she's going to throw her leg up on the table and start gnawing on it.

"I thought you were on the Oprah diet," Lizzy says, double chin resting on palm.

"Ancient history," Max says as she vacuums up her tomato basil sauce. Sticking out her tongue, she picks off an angel hair pasta noodle and drops it on the floor.

There isn't a diet Max hasn't starved herself on. Her latest battle against the bulge is the Simply Red diet.

"You can eat anything as long as it's red," Max says, tossing a handful of red M&M's into her mouth and sucking the "melt in your mouth, not in your hand" candy shell like she's on life support.

The best we can tell, she hasn't lost an ounce, but she could suck the paint off a Chrysler.

Suddenly Max sits straight up in our booth. "Good Gawd," she gasps.

We follow Max's subtle gawk to the restaurant doorway. It takes a couple of minutes to figure out exactly who we're staring at. It kind of looks like Mindy, only a skinnier version.

"Where's the rest of you?" Lizzy asks as Mindy slinks into the chair beside me.

"Size 6," Mindy says, crossing her cellulite-free legs.

"How?" Maxine demands.

"Eat less. Exercise more." Mindy shrugs.

Eyes narrowed, Max glares at her. "No, really."

Picking a cucumber out of my salad, Mindy wipes the dressing onto her napkin.

"Just ice water," she says to the young waiter, waving the menu away.

Mouth open and menu suspended in the air, the waiter just stands there, staring at Mindy's legs.

Snatching the menu out of his hand, Maxine smacks him with it.

"Jerry said if I got down to what I weighed on our wedding day," Mindy explains, "he'd take me to Bermuda."

Lizzy and I roll eyes at each other. The old "weight when I met you" ploy. Been there. Done that.

"A guy can have a hairline that starts at his tailbone," Lizzy says, shaking her head with disgust, "but the minute a woman gets the slightest bit plump, he treats her like meat that's expired."

"I know there are diet drugs in here somewhere," Max mutters as she scratches through Mindy's purse.

"So how much did he *think* you weighed when he married you?" I ask, smirking behind the whipped cream on my café caramel.

"See," Mindy says, pointing with the remains of the cucumber, "there's the problem."

"So what you're telling me is, you *lied* to your future husband," Lizzy says.

"I didn't lie," Mindy says. "I told him my correct weight—only in kilograms."

"Well, you look great," I say. "You're the picture of health."

"And look a decade younger," Lizzy chimes in.

A silence falls over the table as this fact sinks in like a knife in the back.

"So," Lizzy says, pushing her plate across the table, "how 'bout a little cheesecake?"

We women have to stick together. And they haven't invented a better adhesive than cheesecake.

Cracker Jacks

"If Harold ever tries to leave me," Maxine says, "he'll wish he never left the womb."

Nothing maintains matrimony like the fear of having to move back in with mama.

Leila, Maxine, and I are sitting in the waiting room of Rosie's lawyer's office. After nearly twenty years of marriage, Rosie and her soon-to-be-ex are trying to come to a civilized property settlement. They've just spent the past thirty minutes clawing each other's eyes out over the Dirt Devil minivac.

At $150 per hour per lawyer, Rosie and her husband apparently have a real affinity for things that suck.

"Coffee?" the receptionist asks as he sets a tray on the table in front of us.

I personally judge a lawyer by the coffee he serves. If he hands me a jar of Folger's Crystals, I figure Ivana Trump probably doesn't have him on her Rolodex.

"Wow," I say, sniffing the pot, "it smells like . . ."

"Kona," the receptionist says snootily as he fills our cups. "Mr. Mitchell has it flown in weekly from Kauai."

I have no doubt Rosie's husband will be sucking through a straw and squeaking soprano by the time Mr. Mitchell gets through with him.

"How long do these property settlements usually take?" Leila asks, stirring her Kona.

"Oh, they can go on for years," the receptionist says as he adjusts his yellow tie in the reflection of the coffeepot.

"But by the grace of a killer prenup go I," Max says. "If Harold ever tries to divorce me, I get the gold in his teeth."

Setting the coffeepot on the warmer, the receptionist goes to his computer and starts pecking away like Perry Mason's secretary with a five o'clock shadow.

"Has Rosie lost some weight?" Max frowns.

Leila and I follow Max's gawk to the conference room window.

"Is that a new suit?" I ask.

"Is that a new hairstyle?" Leila squints.

"The new hairstyle was my idea," the receptionist chirps, without missing a beat on his keyboard. "Makes her look ten years younger, don't ya think?"

Max, Leila, and I all lean toward the glass. All in all, Rosie hasn't looked this hot since her wedding day. Spouses are like houses. They never look as good as right before they go on the market.

"I wouldn't kick Rosie's old man outta the boardroom either," Max grunts as she tears open a box of Cracker Jacks with her teeth.

"He always was a good-looking man," Leila sighs. "Pure scum, but good-looking."

"*That* was her first mistake," Max says knowingly. "Drive a Yugo and you'll never get car-jacked. I couldn't give my Harold away."

On that note, the receptionist glances up from his computer screen at Max.

Tilting her Cracker Jack box over her mouth, Max taps the bottom. Cheeks stuffed to capacity, Max looks like a giant hamster hoarding caramel corn for the winter.

"Yep, the only way old Harold will ever get rid of me" — Max crunches — "is 'Death do us part.' "

Suddenly Max's eyes get the size of saucers. Then she

starts making little noises like a cat trying to cough up a hairball. When she starts turning blue, the receptionist runs around the desk, grabs Max around the waist—which is no small feat—and gives her the Heimlich. On the third try, Max projects the Cracker Jack prize like a grenade launcher clear into the law library.

"Are you okay?!" Leila and I gasp simultaneously.

"No thanks to you two!" Max snaps, slapping us off of her. "I nearly choked to death!"

"Wow!" Leila says to the receptionist as we watch Max, still mumbling to herself, lumber off to claim her prize. "You saved Maxine's life!"

"Yeah," he says. "Whattaya say, we don't mention that to Harold."

Faute de Mieux

According to Sweetie, if dinosaurs died out because of their lack of flexibility, we'll be pumping oil made from middle-aged women any day.

"We have Coke, Diet Coke, Dr Pepper, root beer, Fresca, tea—hot or cold—orange juice, cranberry juice, apple juice, milk, wine, beer, coffee, and V8," Sweetie calls from inside the refrigerator.

"No Snapple?" Samantha says indignantly.

"Did I say Snapple?"

"Are you sure?" she asks, leaning into the refrigerator beside him.

Looking back over his shoulder, Sweetie glares at me.

Sam and I used to work together. About once a year she passes through town on business and pops in for a visit. Sweetie calls it his annual prostate exam.

"I guess I'll just have water, then," Sam says after rearranging my leftovers.

Chucking some ice into a glass, Sweetie runs it under the tap and hands it to her.

"You don't have bottled water?" she asks, frowning at the glass like it's glowing with toxic waste.

Judging by the look on Sweetie's face, the next drink he offers Sam will be self-serve—top of the stairs, on your right, lift the lid.

"*Faute de mieux*," Sam sighs, taking a sip of ice water.

"Folk duh what?" Sweetie frowns.

"*Faute de mieux*," she says. "For lack of anything better."

On that note, Sweetie lights a cigarette. Then—fearing Sam is going to explode and splatter on the furniture—immediately puts it out.

"What is this?" Sam demands, lifting the lid of a steaming pot.

"Black beans," I say as I toss the salad.

"But we're having chicken," she says incredulously. "I always have potatoes with chicken!"

Sam is a CPA. I just assumed beans would be her primary food source.

"And," she adds, checking her watch, "I always eat at six."

Throwing an Idaho in the microwave, I sling some cheese and crackers on a tray and slide them in front of her. At exactly 5:59, she picks one up.

"So, how's work?" I ask as I try to decide whether to use the good dishes or the junk.

"*Faute de mieux*," she shrugs as she perfectly aligns the cheese on the cracker. "We hired a part-time kid to fill your old job."

The good dishes go back into the cabinet.

"Do you ever ask yourself why *you* do all the cooking?" Samantha asks, cracker suspended in the air.

I think it's rather obvious. If Sweetie cooked, we'd starve. Some dogs guard. Some dogs fetch. Sweetie is like a peekapoo. He's mostly ornamental.

The alarm on her wristwatch goes off, and Sam takes a bite of cracker.

"Charles and I always alternated cooking," she munches nostalgically. "I cooked Mondays, Wednesdays, and Fridays. He cooked Tuesdays, Thursdays, and Saturdays."

"What happened on Sundays?" Sweetie asks.

"We ate out," she says.

"What happened to Charles?" I ask.

"He walked out."

The thought having been planted, Sweetie stares longingly at the front door.

"I've given up on men." Sam shrugs. "I feel there is an inadequate return on my investment."

"Sam," I say gently, "have you ever considered being a little more . . . flexible."

"Flexible?"

"Men like flexible," I say, looking at Sweetie to back me up.

"If a man refuses to compromise, he's persistent," Sam fumes indignantly. "If a woman refuses to bend over backward, she's rigid!"

The thought of a woman bending over backward having been planted, Sweetie meditates.

"Well, I am not a bimbo ball of clay!" Sam declares, carefully folding her napkin, then throwing it on the table. "When a man dates me, you can be sure of the reason."

"*Faute de mieux*," Sweetie mutters.

The Jabber Talkie

Some women are like racehorses—their mouths were meant to run.

". . . and that was the year Fred took up turkey hunting. Was that '78 or '79, Fred? It must have been '78 because we were living in Washington, D.C., and I said to Fred, 'Fred, do they have turkeys in D.C.?' "

Sweetie and I have been "dropped in on" by friends. June and Fred pretty much have to sneak up on us. If we see them coming, we go into hiding under the Friendship Protection Program.

". . . and that was the year Fred took up elk hunting. Was that '81 or '82, Fred? It must have been '82 because I was pregnant with Jo-Jo and retaining water like Hoover Dam."

Men do not understand. You lock a woman up with two rug rats and a nine-pound fetus doing push-ups on her bladder, and it's only natural she's going to strike up a conversation with the diaper pail. Sweetie calls this oral incontinence.

I will admit though, June's mouth ran like Secretariat even before she had kids. I was in her wedding and the preacher could hardly get a word in.

"What do you take in your coffee, Fred?" I ask as I fill his mug.

"No cream, no sugar, but half a package of Equal," June says.

No one knows for sure if Fred can talk. It's Sweetie's theory that Fred used to have vocal cords, but they died.

After a couple of hours with June, you feel your ears finally give out. Sweetie, Fred, and I, eyes glazed and feeling a little numb from the babble bombardment, just sit and watch her mouth move.

June doesn't notice. She just keeps chattering away, lips flapping as if they're trying to fly off her face.

". . . Fred was a vegetarian before we got married. Wouldn't kill a fly. Now, I think he'd shoot me if someone would sell him a license."

Judging by the frost on Sweetie's face, he'd be willing to risk the game warden's wrath.

". . . if I didn't know better, I'd think Fred looks for excuses to stay away from home," June laughs as she drives her elbow into Fred's ribs.

Fred's mug hangs in the air.

"Fred," June says, turning to look at her husband. "*I said . . .* if I didn't know better, I'd think you were looking for excuses to stay away from home."

Fred stares straight ahead like a dazed deer caught by headlights.

"Fred?" June frowns.

Slowly tilting his head, Fred closes his eyes, puckers his lips, and starts kissing the air. When he starts giving it the old tongue action, June goes berserk.

"*Fred!*" June yells. "What in the world are you doing?"

"Did you say something, dear?" Fred asks, blinking innocently.

"You never listen to me," June cries.

"Of course I do!" Fred says, giving her a little reassuring squeeze. "I was just thinking about deer season."

The Only Man I Ever Loved
Was Famous Amos

Lizzy never had much luck with men. The truth is, the only guy who never let her down was Famous Amos.

"Good pastry is like a feather pillow," Lizzy says, holding a croissant up to the light. "You long to bury your face in it."

Lizzy used to write like a pirate—passionate, daring, irreverent. She took no prisoners.

She was on her way to winning a Pulitzer when she fell in love with her editor. By the time he got through editing out everything that might offend anyone, Lizzy's writing was reduced to quotation marks, a couple of commas, and the word "longingly."

"I'll start with Boston Bibb salad with blue cheese dressing," Lizzy says as she smooths her napkin onto her lap.

"You mean raspberry vinaigrette," the waiter corrects as he writes.

Eyes narrowed, Lizzy gives the waiter a searing look.

"A waiter is like a lobster," she says dryly. "Don't bring it to the table if it's still making noise."

After her editor dumped her for the horoscope columnist, they found Lizzy in the dark room castrating anatomically correct newspaper dolls.

"Are your steaks from the rain forest?" Lizzy asks as she studies her menu.

Our waiter looks up from his pad.

"And I would know this be-caaaussse . . . they're wearing little raincoats?"

Lizzy finally found peace that passeth all understanding in the dairy section. She developed a fatal attraction to Ben and Jerry and gained fifty-five pounds. On the positive side, her column on cuisine is more popular than Stove Top stuffing.

"I'm not finished," Lizzy says as the waiter reaches for her salad plate.

"Trust me, darling," he says. "It's over."

"Touch it," Lizzy snarls, "and I'll fillet you like a boneless chicken."

Finally, free to write unbridled, Lizzy blossomed like an onion loaf. Now she's so famous, she's on a first-name basis with Oprah.

"Waiter!" Lizzy bellows.

As she waves her arm, the loose skin flaps like a flag and nearly blows out the candles.

Taking his own sweet time, our waiter finally saunters over to our table. "You bellowed?" he asks.

"Feel this butter!" Lizzy demands.

Glaring at her, our waiter drives his finger into the butter bowl.

"What do you feel?" she asks.

"Your brain on MSG?"

"You feel *cold*," she says. "Butter should be served at room temperature."

Resting both her chins on her laced pudgy fingers, Lizzy gets reflective. "Butter should spread across the flaky flesh of a steaming roll like whipped cream melting on a man's warm chest." Lizzy pauses to take a sip of water. "It should form a glistening rivulet that streams down the valley of his ribs, coming to a warm creamy pool in the concave of his taut belly."

Our waiter is so quiet, you could hear steamed rice fall on the carpet. "What total manure," he finally says.

"Yes, sweetheart, but it's *syndicated* manure."

Wadding his dish towel into a ball, the waiter throws it on the floor and storms off.

"That guy's really a lousy waiter," I note as I wind angel hair pasta around my fork.

"You should have had him for an editor," Lizzy huffs.

Getting Personal

You know you've been out of the dating scene a while when you think DWM is a German car.

"Okay, how about this one?" Maxine asks, spreading the newspaper open on Rosie's kitchen table. "DWM ISO SWF . . ."

"Divorced white male in search of single white female," Leila translates, using the key at the top of the personal ads.

Maxine reads on: ". . . who loves music, movies, and being tied up for indefinite periods of time."

"Actually," Rosie says as she dips her tea bag, "I'd rather not date a guy who's divorced. They can be so bitter." This from the woman whose soon-to-be-ex-husband is currently living in a discarded refrigerator box and subsisting on cat food.

Separated after twenty-two years of marriage, Rosie is about to rejoin the dating game. We're fairly certain that Snow White's Bluebird of Happiness is about to get plucked.

"I don't know about meeting men through the personals." Rosie frowns.

"Really." Leila nods. "What if he's an oversexed Neanderthal who only wants to ravage your body for days at a time?"

Cuddling our mugs, we give this some thought.

"Let me see that thing," Leila says, jerking the paper out of Maxine's hands.

"Louise met her husband through the personals," Maxine says as she shovels sugar into her cup.

"Really?" Rosie asks, perking up.

"Yep," Maxine quips brightly. "Both of them."

"This guy says he's tired of head games," Leila reads.

"What a wuss," Maxine huffs. "My Harold only has three brain cells left, and still he plays on."

"Based on these ads," Leila goes on, "the ideal woman loves the outdoors, just can't get enough baseball, and is a spinner."

Maxine, Leila, and I study Rosie.

Strike one . . . Strike two . . . Strike three, she's out.

"What does it say about the ideal man?" I ask, reading over Leila's shoulder.

"Basically, he's warm-blooded and not living in the back-seat of his car."

Rosie's egg timer buzzes and she goes to add softener to her rinse cycle. As soon as she's out of range, we huddle over a plate of vegetables carved into animals. Kind of your produce menagerie.

"We really need to get Rosie out of the house," I whisper, picking up a zucchini zebra.

You show me a woman who carves happy faces on radishes, and I'll show you a woman spending way too much time alone with her vegetable crisper.

"Surely we know someone she can go out with," Leila whispers.

"I hear they have a really *hot* singles group at the synagogue," Maxine says, crunching on a carrot parrot.

"She's a Presbyterian," Leila whispers.

"Hey!" Maxine snaps. "Show me where it says, 'Thou shalt not change religions to meet men!'"

Rosie drops the clothes hamper on the floor beside us, and we each grab a towel.

"You know," Rosie says as she refolds the washcloth Maxine just folded, "dating isn't what it used to be."

"Yeah," Maxine sighs nostalgically. "Back in my day, we met men the old-fashioned way. We picked them up in fern bars."

Those were the days. Many a match was made at the fix-it-yourself, all-you-can-eat nacho buffet.

Rosie's March

According to Rosie, machines are like men. No matter how much you pamper them, their performance never quite lives up to the hype. Most of the time you'd be better off doing it by hand.

It's Saturday night and my girlfriends and I are headed home after a day of shopping in Atlanta. There isn't a square inch of Rosie's Mercedes that isn't stacked, packed, or crammed. I have a whole new respect for Maxine. This woman can do damage to a mall that makes Sherman's March look like a milk run to the 7-Eleven.

"Everybody all right back there?" Rosie says to her rearview mirror.

There's a muffled sound from the backseat and one of the Saks Fifth Avenue bags rattles. We take this to mean Maxine and Leila haven't suffocated under their plunder.

We're sitting at a stoplight on Peachtree when I first notice the odor.

"Did one of you drop a bottle of something back there?" I call to the backseat. It smells a lot like metal melting, but with today's perfumes, you never know.

The Saks Fifth Avenue bag shakes its handles.

"I think something's wrong with the car," I say, rolling down the window.

About this time, the engine starts knocking like Whitney's cotton gin. We barely make it to the curb before the Mercedes heaves its final breath.

"When was the last time you changed the oil?" Big Ed the mechanic asks as we stare at the engine.

"Change the oil?" Rosie frowns. "You mean, like a deep fat fryer?"

Rosie has never had much luck with anything mechanical. She was the only kid I knew whose Chatty Cathy doll had a stutter.

And ever since her husband left, things have really started falling apart. Slowly but surely, every mechanical device in her house has died a slow, painful death.

Big Ed holds the dipstick to the light and it glitters like stardust. Wiping their hands on shop cloths, the other mechanics at the garage peel their eyes off Leila's legs long enough to check it out.

"Hot Hoover dam," Bill T. says as Bobby whistles as if Cindy Crawford just walked through the garage door wearing nothing but a teddy and a smile.

"I have a feelin', ma'am, this ain't gonna be pretty," Big Ed says, rubbing the metal flecks between his fingers.

"What does that mean?" Rosie asks, turning to me.

"I think it means you've blown the engine," I say.

"What does *that* mean?" Rosie asks, turning to Maxine.

"Sorry, Miz Scarlet, I don't know nuthin' 'bout blowin' no engines." Maxine shrugs.

"It means *big* bucks," Leila says, popping the top on an RC Cola.

Rosie's eyes slowly narrow. If she had a temperature gauge, the little needle would definitely be in the red.

"This is all *his* fault," she steams. "*He* always took care of the cars!"

In Rosie's world, losing a husband is like having the lifetime service contract on all her appliances rendered void.

"Give me that thing!" Rosie hisses, jerking the dipstick away from Big Ed.

Metallic oil dripping down her arm, she holds the dipstick in the air. "As God is my witness, I will *never* be dependent on a man again!" Rosie declares. "Now, somebody show me where to stick this thing!"

The men take a giant step back.

Faithful

"If you dream about another man," Gloria says, "is that being unfaithful?"

Taking a sip of coffee, Leila gives this some thought.

"Are you wired?" she asks.

Gloria was never the sharpest blade in the drawer, but ever since her husband decided to run for public office, she's really starting to scare us.

Kat, Leila, and I are scattered around Gloria's dining room table, helping her stuff envelopes and lick stamps for her husband's political campaign. Knowing Kat, she doesn't have a clue what we're doing. She's just here for the glue.

"I really feel guilty," Gloria sighs as she drops a box of fliers on the table.

"Well, I wouldn't worry about it," Kat says, running her tongue along an envelope. "They can't arrest you for dreaming about it."

"What would the world be like if you couldn't dream about sex?" Leila ponders as she aligns a mailing label on the front of an envelope.

"Daniel says I can't use the *sex* word until after the election," Gloria says. "If he gets elected, I'll never be able to use it again."

When people run for office, the last thing they want is a mate's mouth running behind them.

"If you dreamed about another man," Gloria asks as she folds a flier, "would you tell Sweetie?"

"Absolutely," I say without hesitation.

Nothing makes Sweetie happier than a good bedtime story.

"Maybe I should tell Daniel," Gloria says as she stuffs the flier in an envelope.

"Absolutely not," we say in unison.

Ask yourself, does a guy running for road supervisor really want to know his wife is cruising down dream highway with her top down? Poor Gloria could end up an integral part of the passing lane on I-24.

"It's this election," Gloria says, rubbing her temples. "It's driving me crazy."

There's absolutely no way Sweetie or I could ever run for office. We've done more things at the produce counter than most politicians have done in the privacy of the Oval Office.

"We can't control who we dream about," Leila says, peeling off an address label. "Trust me, I've tried."

"I can," Kat says as her tongue flicks the glue off an envelope like a kitten lapping milk. "When I eat french fries in bed, I always dream about Ronald McDonald."

"Katie, honey," Leila says as she slides Kat's envelopes out of reach, "I think maybe you better fold for a while."

"How often are you having this dream?" I ask as I slap a stamp on an envelope.

"Every night," Gloria says.

Now this gets our attention.

"Sometimes," she whispers, leaning close, "twice!"

"My, my," Leila says, fanning herself with a flier.

"So, who is this hot dream boy of yours?" I ask.

Red pops out on Gloria's cheeks like a turkey thermometer.

"Oh . . . no one," she mumbles, nervously shuffling envelopes like a Vegas blackjack dealer.

Leila and I roll eyes at each other. Kat's eyes are rolling, but without any particular destination.

"If you cooperate," Leila says, "you'll receive full immunity."

Biting her lip, Gloria stares at us.

"Oh, all right!" she blurts. "It's Al Gore!"

"Oh, I dream about him all the time," Kat says, waving her hand.

"Me too," Leila admits with a shrug.

Kat, Leila, and Gloria turn to stare at me.

"Kinda puts a whole new spin on global warming, doesn't it?" I say.

Desperate Women
and
Hairless Chihuahuas

I never really understood the deal about Samson's strength being in his hair until all the guys I know started losing theirs.

Gritting his teeth, the man at the table next to mine suddenly grabs his scalp with both hands and pulls as hard as he can. "Aaaaagh!" he screams.

As a rule, I try not to stick my nose into other people's business. But if this guy is dying from food poisoning, I may want to rethink the blackened salmon.

"I'm stretching my scalp," the man explains as he greases his head with Mother's Friend anti-stretch-mark cream.

There isn't a woman in the world who isn't familiar with the concept of stretching. We are, after all, the sex that perfected cramming a size 8 foot into a size 7 shoe. But leave it to a man to try and take it to a higher level.

"Why?" I ask, taking a sip of coffee.

"Why?!" he crows in disbelief. "Because women don't date bald guys!"

Personally, I'm more of a chest-hair kinda girl. To me a good man is like a mug of beer. The head is strictly ornamental.

"You have no idea what it's like to be bald," he says bitterly. "I'm smart, well read, a blast to be with, but women won't give me the time of day."

I'm sure the baggy scalp skin drooping on top of his head like a mushroom cap has absolutely nothing to do with it.

"So," he says, flipping his napkin into his lap, "I'm getting a hair transplant."

Isn't it interesting that a man has no trouble transplanting hair from one part of his body to another, but goes berserk when you ask him to push a couch across the room.

"First, they surgically remove the loose, hairless skin . . ." he explains graphically as he polishes his steak knife with his napkin.

I'm thinking he's a little old for this, but I don't want to give the poor guy an age complex on top of the bald thing.

" . . . then they stretch the hair from the back of the head to the front," he says.

"Oh, ouch!" I cringe. "That's gotta hurt."

"We're talking fifty thousand bucks." He nods.

"Does your insurance cover this?" I ask.

"Are you kidding?" he huffs, rolling his eyes. "They'll pay for the Viagra after you get a woman, but they don't do a blasted thing to help you bag one."

Darn those HMOs.

"Will you have to sell your house to pay for the operation?" I ask.

"Well, no . . . ." He frowns.

"Honey," I say, patting his hand knowingly, "a man with fifty grand to transplant hair who can't find a date hasn't fully explored all his assets."

"So," he says, leaning forward, "are you seeing someone?"

After two decades together, Sweetie and I have entered our "blind salamander phase." We haven't actually seen each other since the eighties, but somehow we still manage to find each other in the dark.

"Look," I say, reaching into my knapsack, "I have a friend who would love you."

Pulling out my Rolodex of single girlfriends, I flip past "as long as he's still breathing" to the "hair optional" section.

"She's the greatest," I assure him as I jot Rosie's name and number on a napkin. "She's smart, well read, a blast to be with . . ."

Baldie stares at the napkin. "She's fat, isn't she?" he says.

"I wouldn't call her fat," I say, biting my lip.

"I may be bald," he sniffs, arms crossed and chin in the air, "but I'm not desperate!"

On that note, I snatch the napkin off the table. Rosie may be temporarily desperate, but even with a hair transplant, this guy will always be a little hairless Chihuahua.

Mother Goose

Once upon a time Mindy was *hot*. She had more guys chasing after her skirt than Snow White. Then she met Prince Charming, hatched two kids, and turned into Mother Goose. Now she quacks senselessly all day and has a fluffy white tail that waggles when she waddles.

"Where's your mom?" I ask.

"With Daddy," Kid says, not looking up from his Game Boy video game.

"So where's your dad?" I ask.

"In the nursery," he says.

"Your mouth is blue," I say.

"It is not!" Kid says, scrubbing his lips with his sleeve.

Classic case of raspberry Dum-Dum denial.

Suddenly our intellectually stimulating conversation is interrupted by a snap, crackle, and pop coming from the kitchen counter.

"What's that?" I ask.

Kid rolls his eyes at my lameness. "BabyCom," he huffs.

Barfing your brains out for nine months and having your skin stretched to the size of the Astrodome seem a small price to pay for the rewards of this little bundle of joy.

"Are you my precious baby?" Mindy's voice suddenly echoes through the BabyCom speaker.

I picture Mindy and Jerry, washed in a golden ray of heavenly light, standing over the baby's crib, staring down in awe at the tiny miracle they have created together—the Biscuit.

"Have you been a good boy?" Mindy baby-talks.

About this time there's a rustle in the playpen next to the kitchen table. From underneath a pile of baby blankets, dressed in OshKosh B'Gosh's finest, emerges the Biscuit. Pulling his biscuit-dough body to a standing position, he clings to the bumper pad with one hand and stuffs his other fist into his mouth. With eyes the size of VW headlights, he stares at BabyCom.

No doubt when the Biscuit grows up he'll spend years in therapy for having an Oedipal complex with small speakers.

"I think you've been a very . . . verrry . . . baaad boy," Mindy growls.

It suddenly dawns on me that Mother Goose and Daffy Daddy Duck are about to go "Wee! Wee! Wee!" all the way home.

"Where's the volume control?" I yell over the "Oh, baby!" thundering from BabyCom.

"Why?" Kid asks. "You want to turn it up?"

"OH, MAMA!" Jerry screams.

Grabbing BabyCom, I throw it in the dishwasher, kick the door closed, and spin the dial to Rinse and Hold.

Falling back against the counter, I look up. Kid and the Biscuit are staring at me like I just drowned Barney.

And the moral of this story is, just because a woman walks like a duck and talks like a duck, doesn't mean she can't still cook like a microwave oven.

The Boxer

According to Sweetie, life is like a boxing match. You gotta
stay on your toes, deflect the blows, and when some guy bites
your ear off—pick up the pieces.

"Why do these things happen to me?" Rosie asks, flat on
her back and staring up at her living room ceiling.

This morning Rosie was notified via certified mail that
she's being sued by her new neighbor across the street.

"He slipped on the grease spot," Leila explains as she reads
the letter from the lawyer.

The infamous grease spot is a memento of Rosie's marriage. When Rosie's ex-husband hit male menopause, he
bought a Porsche—then promptly rode off into the sunset with
a twenty-four-year-old dental hygienist with perfect teeth.

Another little moral here: never let a hussy look your husband in the mouth.

"We have a name; we have an address," Maxine says, glaring at Rosie's neighbor's house through the bay window. "I say
we go stomp the wimp's pansy bed!"

During times of crisis, men are not the only ones who
want to flatten the landscape. I figure we women will be a
force to contend with—just as soon as we start thinking on a
slightly grander scale.

"It's probably just a misunderstanding," Leila says as she
scans the letter.

Leila's former brother-in-law is a lawyer. We trust her legal advice completely.

"It's been my experience that bad luck comes in threes," Rosie says, ". . . or multiples of threes."

"Nothing that can't be resolved," Leila assures us, still reading.

". . . or nines," Rosie says as she stares into space, ". . . or multiples of nines."

"Well," Leila finally sighs, looking up from the letter, "they can't take your health."

On that note, Rosie's body draws up into the fetal position.

There's nothing harder than watching your friend go down for the count. In Rosie's world, men do not sue women, and when a woman says, "I do," the obituary will read, "survived by his spouse."

Ripping open a bag of Keebler's with her teeth, Max grabs a handful, then passes the bag. You know Rosie's in bad shape when she serves store-bought cookies.

"Cut to the chase," Max says, with her mouth full. "What's the worst that can happen?"

"She could lose everything," Leila shrugs, dipping into the bag for a Sandie.

Chewing, Max does a quick inventory of the house—before the other buzzards start pulling up in U-Hauls.

"Why do these things happen to me?" Rosie mutters in dazed disbelief.

"Because you're a wuss," Max says matter-of-factly. "The world eats women like you for breakfast."

Max never pulls any punches. Of course, if you said something like that to her, she'd write your phone number on the wall in the Greyhound bus station men's room.

Rosie stares at me like a woman who's lost her religion. Superman is not coming to save the day or to fix her major appliances.

I used to wonder why my mother's friends looked so defeated and dull-eyed, knocked to their knees by the simple act of living. I never thought it would happen to us. But then, I never thought we'd have crow's-feet either.

"Honey," I say gently, "a girl can either get sad or get mad."

Leila, Maxine, and I stand at the bay window and watch Rosie jumping up and down in her neighbor's pansies.

"Didn't Rosie plant those pansies as a housewarming gift?" Leila asks.

Life is like a boxing match. We women haven't quite got the rules down yet, but anybody who takes a swing at us is going to end up with a lotta dead pansies.

Bony

"How many times has he been married?" Rosie asks.

When you reach our age, dating is like a used-car lot. They've all been previously owned. You just hope it wasn't by Rent-a-Wreck.

"Only twice," Maxine assures her.

"What happened the first time?" Rosie asks.

"They outgrew each other." Max nods knowingly.

Translation: His wife traded up.

Rosie is now officially divorced and the universe is uneasy. Apparently, there's an unwritten law that states a divorced woman is a void that must be filled. And as far as Max is concerned, she's found the perfect man to fill it. He's single. He's heterosexual. And he's standing in the driveway.

"Does he have any children?" Rosie asks, taking a peek over the porch rail at her intended.

"They're practically grown," Max says, with a drop of the wrist.

Translation: Little Robert, Jr., needs only minimal assistance to get off the potty seat.

Maxine, Rosie, and I are sitting on my front porch. We each have a bagful of sugar snap peas at our feet and newspapers in our laps. Like synchronized swimmers, we pinch the stems off, pull the strings, and toss the peas into a bowl.

"You know you can buy these frozen," Max grumbles as she reaches down for another fistful of peas. "Ready to nuke."

I roll my eyes in disgust. You have to wonder about a woman who cannot distinguish between a pea that's fresh from the garden and one that comes hermetically sealed. I have long suspected that Maxine has an Adam's apple waiting to come out.

"I could never love a bony man," Rosie says as she nibbles on a raw pea.

Max and I follow Rosie's stare to the driveway. At Max's prompting, Sweetie and Robert are bent over Rosie's Mercedes checking the antifreeze. It's Max's theory that a man never looks more appealing than when performing free car maintenance.

"He isn't bony," Max insists. "He's stylishly thin, like Hugh Grant."

The truth is, Robert is a human fire pole. If you tried to hug him, you'd slide to the floor and end up in a lip lock with the linoleum.

Rosie shakes her head in doubt. "I could never marry a man whose thighs are thinner than mine," she says firmly.

Max and I do an involuntary scan of Rosie's thighs. They're oozing over the sides of the Adirondack like creamy butter frosting. This definitely narrows the field.

"Honey," Max says matter-of-factly, "either you're going to have to lower your standards just a tad, or your next American Express card will have MRS. P. DOUGHBOY stamped across the bottom."

"I was really hoping to find a nice widower," Rosie sighs. "Divorced men have so much baggage."

"Trust me," Max says dryly. "Your trunk can handle it."

Rosie stares down at the pile of pea hulls in her lap as though she'd like to crawl on top of them.

"Rosie," I say gently, "there's no rule that says you have to be married."

"You're telling me you'd give up men," Max huffs skeptically.

Well, now, I didn't say that.

"If Sweetie left you," Rosie asks, forehead furled, "would you marry another man?"

I glance off the porch at Sweetie. Even after all these years, the boy still rings my dinner bell. "I couldn't go back to eating frozen peas," I say.

"Then again," Rosie says as she gives Robert a little wave, "throw a little fat on them, and you can barely tell the difference."

Rosie's First Date

According to Sweetie, a woman may look like she has low mileage, but you never know what kind of wreck is underneath the paint job.

"How much time do we have?" Maxine asks as she dumps a suitcase of cosmetics onto the bathroom countertop.

"He's picking her up in two hours," I say, glancing at the clock.

Lifting Rosie's head out of the toilet, Max surveys the damage.

"I won't make any guarantees," Max says, "but we'll do what we can do."

Rosie is about to go on her first date in ten years. The bad news is, she's having a nervous breakdown. The good news is that—having worshiped at the porcelain throne for two days—she's at least five pounds thinner.

"Men are totally dishonest," Rosie mutters as Max polishes her fiberglass-sculpted nails and I dye her gray hair with Miss Clairol, Sienna Red.

"Wow," I say as I study Rosie's roots. "I had no idea you were a brunette."

"I am?" Rosie says, leaning toward the mirror and squinting at the part in her hair. Without her hazel-tinted contact lenses, Rosie can't find the nose job on her face.

"Every night I go to bed and pray I'll wake up gay," Rosie mutters.

"We should all be so lucky," Max says as she shoves Rosie's face into a sink of ice water to achieve the flushed look. When Rosie comes up for air, she looks like a cabin boy on the *Titanic*.

"She's blue," I say as I chip the ice off.

"A thick coat of foundation will take care of it," Max assures me as she tweezes Rosie's eyebrows like she's plucking a chicken.

"Men are never what they seem!" Rosie cries hysterically.

"Tell us something we don't know," Max snorts as she slaps a base coat of anti-aging cream on Rosie, followed by concealer to hide the bags, moisturizing foundation with a light refractor to erase the crow's-feet, blush on the apple of the cheek to give that youthful glow, and a light dusting of translucent powder.

"Well?" Max asks.

"Very natural," I say.

Eyebrows knitted, Max studies Rosie like Picasso. Then, dipping her brush onto a palette of eye shadows, Max proceeds to paint a couple of eyes onto Rosie's blank face.

"By extending the color outside the mouth," Max says, biting her lip gloss in concentration as she outlines Rosie's lip with lip liner, "you can achieve that pouty 'just pumped full of silicone' effect."

While I unwrap the towel around Rosie's red head, Max pulls out the Harley-Davidson of hair dryers. Put handles on this baby, and you could ride her.

Gripping the dryer with both hands, Max nods and I plug it in. A blast of red-hot air shoots out like jet exhaust. What hair isn't blown off Rosie's head is left standing straight up in the carefree "bed head" style.

Mumbling incoherently, Rosie jiggles herself into her Miracle Bra.

"Talk about making a mountain out of a couple of mole-hills," Max whistles in awe.

"I read that this material was developed by the defense department," I grunt as Max and I stuff Rosie into her new rib-to-ankle featherlight girdle.

"And they said Star Wars was a waste of taxpayer money," Max huffs as she pokes a pooch in with the hairbrush handle.

Finally, our work is done. Taking a deep breath, Rosie does a slow turn for us to inspect the final product.

"Rosie," I say, "words fail me."

"Remember, honey," Max says, patting Rosie on her shoulder pad, "just be yourself."

The Nut Doesn't Fall Far from the Family Tree

Pickles

"Well, you don't have to worry about me," Mom says, shoulders slumped. "When the time comes, I'll get a little room with a hot plate and a percolator, and I'll be just fine."

Sis and I roll eyes at each other.

Ever since Mom went to visit her friend in the nursing home, she's been treating us like we're going to stuff her into a pull-tight Hefty and haul her down to the landfill.

"Mother," Sis says, "you'll outlive us all."

"Primarily because you're going to irritate us to death before our time," I add.

Under normal circumstances, Sis would be peeling my tongue-lashed body off the wall right about now. But today Mom just stares out the window.

"Do you know what people do with their elderly parents in New York City?" Mom asks as the waitress sets another bowl of Polish pickles down in front of her.

"Trade them to the Cubs?" I ask, taking a sip of coffee.

"They drive them into the country and drop them off like dogs," Mom says sadly.

Taking a long drag off her cigarette, Sis gives this some thought. "Don't they have places for unwanted parents?" Sis asks. "You know, like a dog pound for parents?"

"Home run," I mouth, swinging my imaginary bat.

"In the old days," Mom says as she sadly crunches into a pickle, "people respected their elders."

"In the old days," I say, "Arctic tribes left their parents on icebergs and floated them out to sea."

"But I'm sure they were very respectful about it," Sis adds, blowing smoke out of the corner of her mouth.

"Maybe I'll become a nun," Mom sighs.

"A nun," I nod.

Mom is wearing two-inch spiked heels, pedal pushers, and a ruffled top. The only order of nuns she could get into would be the Holy Sisters of the Chiquita Banana.

Snapping open her purse, Mom pulls out a ragged lipstick-smudged Kleenex and dabs her eyes. No doubt it's the same Kleenex she used at my high school graduation.

Chins resting in our palms, Sis and I watch as Mom carefully unfolds a crumpled wad of tinfoil and proceeds to rub it flat on the table.

"Mom," I finally ask, "what are you doing?"

Picking up the dish of pickles, Mom dumps them onto the tinfoil.

"I take it they don't have Polish dills in your grocery," I say.

"I'm embarrassing my daughters," my mother informs the table next to us.

"You're going to get pickle juice all over everything," I insist.

"I wiped this kid's butt," Mom broadcasts across the restaurant as she reaches across the table and stabs the remains of my kosher, "and she's complaining about pickle juice."

"Mother, I will buy you a jar of pickles."

"This is how it starts," she bellows. "First they throw away the pickles! Then they throw away the mother!"

"I should have joined the Peace Corps when I had the chance," I mumble.

Standing up, Mom leans into my face. "Young lady," she growls, eyebrow arched, "you're still not too big for me to bend over my knee."

"I don't know," Sis says, eyeballing my behind. "It's borderline."

"I'll bury you both!" Mom declares as she storms across the restaurant, waving a handful of stolen Equal and dripping a trail of pickle juice.

"Now, that's the woman we know and love," Sis says proudly.

The Ghost of Elvis

"The first time we saw Elvis's ghost, he was sittin' right there," Earl says, pointing to the dining room table behind the velvet ropes. "He was eatin' meatloaf."

Earl and Reba look so much like a young Elvis and Priscilla, it's spooky. Earl has sleepy bedroom eyes, and if Reba is ever in a tornado, I have no doubt her hair will be the only thing left standing.

"Do you guys always dress like this?" I ask.

"Like whut?" Earl asks, upper lip curled and twitching.

It is my first time to Graceland and, other than the eight-foot stained-glass simulated-sapphire studded peacocks in the living room, it's nowhere near as gaudy as I thought it would be.

Muslims go to Mecca. Jews go to Jerusalem. My people go to Graceland. Elvis is the standard to which all us white trash aspire. He's like white compost.

"Do you think we'll see Elvis's ghost today?" I ask.

"He don't show himself to just anybody," Earl says.

"You gotta be worthy," Reba says. "Yer wearin' white cotton underwear, ain't ya?"

You can bet the 700,000 people who make the pilgrimage to Graceland every year won't get this kind of insider information off the self-guided tour tape, available in eight languages.

Stopping at the bottom of the mirrored stairway in the entry hall, Earl and Reba stare up at the blue satin curtain with gold tassels that hangs across the upstairs hall.

"It was his private place," Earl sighs reverently.

When Elvis was alive, fans would hang on the rock wall that surrounds Graceland, trying to get a look at him. Dozens of hangers-on swarmed the lower floors of the house. And so Elvis would hide on the top floor of Graceland, coming out only at night like Anne Frank—or Dracula, depending on your perspective.

"The first time Earl and me came to Graceland was on our honeymoon," Reba reminisces as we stroll into the kitchen. "You 'member, Earl?"

"Well, honey, you know I do," Earl says, taking a comb out of his back pocket and running it down both sides of his slicked-back hair. "You wuz pregnant with the boy."

"I was swollen like a tick," Reba sighs, resting her hand on her authentic Graceland T-shirt.

"Her water broke right beside that two-tiered trellis of wax fruit," Earl says, pointing.

"They let us finish the tour the next day," Reba assures me.

"Did you see Elvis that year?" I ask.

"Naw," Earl says, shaking his hips. "I figure the birthin' musta put him off."

Reba and Earl bend down to inspect a grease spot on the kitchen counter.

"Fried chicken," Earl says, sniffing the Formica like a bloodhound. "He's done been here."

The presence of Elvis does feel strong in this room. That or the psychedelic orange and lime green carpet is making me nauseous.

"After Priscilla became a mama, Elvis stopped havin' marital relations with her," Reba says, rolling an accusing eye toward Earl. "He held her in too high a regard."

"Now, bay-buh," Earl says, "we done been over this. If I had Marilyn Monroe curled up next tuh me in a '56 metallic purple Cadillac convertible, I could regard *you* high, too."

"You saw Marilyn's ghost with Elvis?" I ask.

"Well, you did know her and President John F. Kennedy broke up," Reba says, as serious as "Heartbreak Hotel."

While Earl covets Elvis's twenty-four-karat eighth-degree-black-belt karate ring, Reba and I check out a video of his concerts.

"That's one hunka hunka burnin' love," Reba shivers as we watch a young Elvis, in black leather, bump and grind.

Generally I go for the dark, intellectual types, but I can appreciate Elvis's raw animal magnetism. I wouldn't kick him out of the jungle room.

All too soon we reach the end of our tour of Graceland, and still no sign of The King.

Elvis has sold over one billion records worldwide. He made thirty-three movies, shook hands with presidents, jammed with the Beatles, and died at forty-two. His grave is forever covered with flowers and lit by an eternal torch that burns night and day.

Tears in her eyes, Reba reaches into her purse, pulls out a peanut butter and jelly sandwich—his favorite—and carefully places it on his monument.

Suddenly, in the distance, walking barefoot across the grass with a daisy in his hand, I see him. "Oh, my gosh!" I gasp, wagging my finger. "It's . . . it's . . . John Lennon!"

"Him? Hell, he's here every year," Earl says, blowing it off with a wave of the hand. "We thought he wuz the yard boy."

The Gravy Boat

"No one can fry a chicken like you, May," my great-uncle Franklin declares as he does a little Polygrip chatter to reseat his dentures.

It's Sunday dinner and my great-aunt May has been burning up the kitchen since Thursday. Baked ham, roast beef, and fried chicken stretch for as far as the eye can see. Aunt May is of the old school—a serving of every species.

"Have another piece of caramel pie, Franklin," Aunt May chirps.

Franklin proceeds to shovel pie onto his plate like he's digging out coal miners.

Every Sunday, Franklin stuffs himself like it's his last meal. And in a way, it is. Franklin's wife, Julia, couldn't put Spam on a cracker with a recipe. At family reunions, you always know which dish Julia brought. Flies won't land on it.

"More iced tea, Franklin?" Aunt May coos.

As Aunt May refills his glass, Franklin gazes up at her like she's the Patron Saint of Corn Oil.

"I think maybe I'll have one more bite of chicken to cut the sweet," Franklin says, stabbing a thigh off the platter, then drowning it in gravy. "I do love your thighs, May," he says, with his mouth full.

"Why, Franklin," Aunt May gushes, "I always suspected

you were a leg man." Batting her cataracts, Aunt May gives Franklin a look that could bake biscuits.

Chest swollen and blushing like a boy, Franklin pats his mustache with a napkin. "Now, if you ladies will excuse me," he crows, reaching for his cane, "I think I'll have my cigar out on the porch." Twirling his cane like a baton, Franklin all but kicks his heels together on his way out the door.

The air in the room is as thick as Aunt May's lumpless gravy. Breathing like a bull about to charge, Cousin Julia glares across the mashed potatoes at Aunt May.

"Vinegary old virgin," Julia hisses. "You've been after my Franklin since I brought him home!"

Which most likely was in a covered wagon.

Wide-eyed, Aunt May perks like an indignant parakeet, then looks at me for reinforcement. I develop a sudden fascination with the wallpaper.

"Why, Julia," Aunt May whimpers, "you have cut me to the quick!"

"Don't play coy with me, May," Julia snaps. "My dead body will still be warm when you come knocking on my door with a tuna casserole!"

Aunt May cringes. She wouldn't be caught dead feeding a man a casserole, much less tuna.

"Well, if you think you'll be dancing on *my* coffin," Cousin Julia declares as she creaks to a stand, "think again!"

Julia is doing a slow totter toward the door when her eyes narrow. Grabbing the gravy boat off the warming table, she lifts it over her head. She's about to send it sailing when Aunt May screams, "Not the gravy boat! It was Grandmother Hilliard's!"

Julia lowers Aunt May's gravy and studies it like it's the cure for liver spots. "I thought *I* had Grandmother Hilliard's china," she frowns.

A silent "Oops" all but wakes the dead. Holding my

breath, I glance over at Aunt May to see if she's preparing to meet her maker. Wide-eyed, Aunt May blinks like a barn owl.

"First you steal my china, then you try to steal my husband!" Fuming, Julia points a bony finger at Aunt May. "If you don't watch yourself, missy, you are going to burn!"

Grabbing her chest, Aunt May gasps with horror. When it comes to burning things, Aunt Julia is an authority.

Midnight

It's after midnight and I'm wide-awake. After two hours of making angels in my sheets, I figure I might as well get up and do something productive.

"Make that a chili dog with cheese and onions, large fries, and a chocolate malt," I yell into the speaker.

"We've got cheddar peppers on sale for ninety-nine cents," the voice cracks over the intercom.

"Oh, why not," I say.

I inherited my "eat yourself to sleep" habit from my dad. Whenever Dad had trouble catching Zs, he'd shake me into a walking coma, put Elvis on the stereo, and we'd cook. His favorite midnight snack was eggs over easy, cold cornbread, dill pickles, and Heineken.

Yes, he is still living.

While I'm waiting for my cellulite-in-a-sack, I check out my fellow feasters. I'm guessing half these kids were just weaned. Instead of straws, they should be sipping from Big Bird training cups.

I'm wiping chili off my chin when a couple of boys in their Dad's Lincoln slide up to the speaker on my left. When they roll down the window to order, the sonic blast of rap sends my malt moonwalking down the dash. I'm not one of those people who put down the next generation's taste, but you have to wonder about music that makes food try to escape.

Apparently, the guys in the jacked-up Chevy feel the need for a cultural exchange. They pump up Smashing Pumpkins to a blue-veined scream, which prompts the girls in the Saturn sedan to stir in a little Spice Girls. (Having been a card-carrying Monkees fan, who am I to judge?)

As much as I'm enjoying the ambience of dueling tweeters, I decide it's time to move on down the highway.

The night is clear as a bell, Creedence Clearwater is on the radio, and the next thing I know I'm clipping down the Natchez Trace headed for Tupelo, Mississippi. When I get to the bridge that spans Highway 96, I decide to pull over to watch the bad moon rising.

This bridge is so high up, you could parachute off of it. Leaning against the car, I stare up at the sky. Junk food, rock and roll, and a warm summer night. If I had a hickey on my neck, it'd be just like high school.

"And that was Creedence Clearwater," the DJ croons, ". . . from 1969."

Did he say 1969? I do a little math in my head and it's all I can do to keep from jumping.

"Is there a problem?" the state trooper asks, having slipped up behind me.

The problem is, he just scared what few years I have left right out of me.

Shining a flashlight in my face, the cop eyes me suspiciously. I'm about to assure him that all I'm doing is torpedoing the pavement below with cheddar peppers when I seem to recall that the penalty for pitching things off a federal bridge is the electric chair.

"Cheddar pepper, Officer?" I ask.

"On sale for ninety-nine," he says, taking two.

If they'd offered those *federales* a couple of tacos, Butch and Sundance would have died in their sleep.

"I couldn't sleep," I explain.

"Guilty conscience," the cop says.

"Never kept me awake before," I say.

The cop stops chewing.

About this time, the DJ spins another oldie. Four haunting plucks of the guitar, and you know it's "Ode to Billy Joe." The music swirls out of the car window and hangs in the sky with the other stars like it belongs there.

"They don't know how to make music like this anymore," the cop says softly.

"It's called progress," I say.

Or lack of talent, depending on one's perspective.

When Bobbie Gentry gets to the chorus, the cop and I join in.

". . . Toda-ay Bil-ly Joe Mac-Al-lis-ter jumped off the Tal-la-hach-cheee bri-iiidge . . . ."

"Wow," the cop says, looking over at me, "you look too young to know that song."

I may never go out in daylight again.

Evening in Paris

It is evening in Paris. Boats glide down the Seine and street-lights cast shadows on lovers strolling along the Champs Elysées. Waving her little flag, our tour guide leads us like baby ducks into a quaint little bistro off the tourist-beaten path.

"I want you to exper-reee-ehnce the trooo fla-verrr of my ceeet-teee," Monique calls back over her shoulder.

Based on the expression of the French patrons as we pass, that would be spit.

Winding forever through the dark smoky room, we finally arrive at our table. Sweetie, coat draped over his shoulders and sunglasses on, misses his chair and lands in my lap.

"The candle's a little bright for you?" I ask dryly.

Throwing his hands up, Sweetie shrugs like he can't understand English. Ever since we skidded to a landing at De Gaulle, Sweetie has been going native. Any minute I'm expecting him to burst into "Thank hea-von for leee-tle girrrls . . . ."

"Now, that we're chummies," Richard says, leaning close, "may I ask you something personal?"

Our first day on the continent, Richard and I had the clams in cream sauce. Nothing like being facedown in a French toilet with a guy to rush a friendship along.

"Sure," I shrug, mouth full of one of those little white bricks the French call bread.

"Besides cutting hair, does your hairstylist moonlight as a butcher?"

Before I know what's hit me, Richard is jerking bobby pins out of my bun and stuffing them in his mouth for safekeeping. Whipping a rat-tail comb and battery-operated curling iron out of his fanny pack, he goes to work.

While I feel very honored having my hair done by the man who assisted with Jennifer Aniston's famous cut, having my face accented with spit strands isn't exactly the aura of mystique I was going for on my first night in Paris.

Meanwhile, Monique and Sweetie are jabbering away in French. They could be talking about septic tanks for all I know.

Sliding a tiny French cigarette from a pack, Monique dangles it in the air. Smooth as pâté, Sweetie whips out his Bic. Or, as they say in France, *Beee-kuh.*

French women are truly amazing. We need to put them in laboratories and study them. I've spent half my life trying to sweep Sweetie off his feet. Monique puts a lip lock on a burning butt and sucks the breath out of him like a Dustbuster.

"Monique," Richard chats as he teases my hair into a cotton candy mountain, "what's your hair routine?"

"Eeeets no-thing, reee-ally." Monique shrugs. "I jooosss wash weeeth . . . how you say . . . soap. Then I shake eeet drrry."

Closing her eyes, Monique arches her head back and tosses her mass of curls to demonstrate.

"Oh, sure you do," Sweetie says skeptically.

Slowly Monique leans across the table. "Come to my rooom to-night," she whispers, eyelids at half mast, "and I show you."

From the waist up, Sweetie is as cool as vichyssoise. Meanwhile, underneath the table, his leg is hammering up and down like Thumper the rabbit.

"Don't take it personally," Richard stage-whispers, nose crinkled. "She's French. If she were all alone, she'd be talking dirty to the butter."

One last pick of my hair, and Richard inspects his creation. "I am a genius!" he squeals, tapping his fingers together under his chin.

Slowly, every French head in the place turns its bored eyes my way. Fortunately, there's so much hair stringing in my face, my mother wouldn't know me.

"Well," Richard says, turning me around to face Sweetie, "what do you think?"

"She looks like Cousin It," Sweetie says.

France gave us Brigitte Bardot and Catherine Deneuve. We gave them Jerry Lewis and the Big Mac. Sort of sums it all up in a bad clam sauce, doesn't it?

Cousin Clara

My family doesn't like to flaunt its good fortune. Too many of our relatives are likely to walk off with it.

"These stay," Aunt May says, lifting a stack of *National Geographics* out of the throwaway box. Tottering across the living room in her ever-stylish orthotic pumps, she drops the magazines on the stairs, right where I found them.

I'm sitting on the floor of my great-aunt May's house, trying to thin out seventy-five years of her life. As fast as I throw something in the box, Aunt May digs it out and puts it back. It's like trying to push water uphill.

"Today's youth are so wasteful," my cousin Clara says absently, a Lucky Strike glued to her lip by an inch of blood-red lipstick. Thumping a crystal goblet, she evaluates the quality of the ring like an appraiser at Sotheby's.

Cousin Clara is supposed to be helping me with this project, but her idea of cleaning up is thinning out the teaspoons in Aunt May's silverware drawer. Clara's our relative and we love her, but basically, the woman's a vulture in lime-green Spandex.

"Aunt May," I say, "why do you need to keep the March 1972 issue of *Reader's Digest?*"

"Suppose next month's issue doesn't come," Aunt May says, thumbing through an article on Nixon's trip to China. "What would I read?"

"There are stores," I say. "You can buy one."

"Duplication of spending is why this country's going to hell in a handbasket," Clara says as she rubs a little silver polish on the bottom of Aunt May's pickle dish.

"You should listen to your cousin," Aunt May says, wagging her finger at me.

I roll my eyes at Clara, but she's too busy counting linen napkins to notice.

It occurs to me that Clara's spending a lot of time with Aunt May lately, and that's not a good sign. You can always tell when a relative's about to kick the bucket. Clara starts circling.

"Aunt May," I ask, "how are you feeling?"

"I'll outlive you all!" Aunt May declares as she drags a box of Sears catalogues back to the closet.

I go back to sorting before she gets down on the floor and starts doing one-arm push-ups.

"What's this?" I ask, pulling a wad of red plastic mesh out of a paper grocery sack.

"They're bags that onions come in," Aunt May says, taking the sack from me. "They're very useful."

"Yeah," I say skeptically, "when was the last time you used one?"

"Clara!" Aunt May cries, pursing her lips and wrapping her arms tightly around the grocery sack, "she's trying to throw my onion sacks away!"

"There, there," Clara says, consoling Aunt May with a hug while taking the opportunity to check out her cameo stickpin. The woman is human Saran Wrap, 100 percent plastic and totally transparent.

"You know," Cousin Clara says to me NutraSweetly as she bites into the silver picture frame holding Great-Uncle Harlan, "I haven't seen your new house yet."

"It's a barn," I say hurriedly, "a mere shack."

"You look pale, dear," Clara says, putting the back of her hand to my forehead. "How are you feeling?"

Amphibians and Other Scum Dwellers

Mom was determined that Sis and I would learn everything there was to know about the birds and the bees at home. She wasn't opposed to their teaching "IT" at school. She just doubted the expertise of my home economics and human development teacher, Miss Hatzmen.

"The woman couldn't mate socks," Mom told Dad after their first parent-teacher conference.

After two years in Miss Hatzmen's class, you came away with the firm belief that the key to a successful marriage was a light and flaky muffin.

While Miss Hatzmen could work herself into a panting sweat discussing tuna melts, anything pertaining to human contact turned her into a frozen fish stick.

Mom, on the other hand, grew up on a farm. This woman knew animal husbandry like Old McDonald knew *eee-i-o*.

"Okay," she'd say as she brushed my hair into a ponytail, "this is how frogs do it."

Then Mom would get into a rousing description of mating amphibians and skin my hair back so tight, my eyes were pulled to slits. I'd have to feel my way to the school bus, where the driver called me Wong Sue. I had a receding hairline by age twelve, but won the math award three years in a row.

In all fairness to Miss Hatzmen, she was playing to a pretty rough crowd. The accessory du jour at our school was the ever-popular fringed leather halter with matching switchblade, and the project that won first place at the science fair was "Home Pregnancy Tests: A Consumer's Report."

"Miss Hatzmen needs a man," Mom announced as she washed, rinsed, and dried a plate, then passed it to me to put in the dishwasher.

A woman could be dangling from a cliff by a bobby pin, and Mom's solution was to find her a date.

"What about your American history teacher?" Mom asked. "He's single."

It was common knowledge that the history teacher and the French teacher had been "conjugating verbs" in the language lab during study hall. Besides, I had my doubts about him. No matter what we were studying, Mr. Wilson always managed to steer the topic toward you-know-what.

"As you can plainly see," he'd say, tracing the map with his pointer, "the land obtained during the Louisiana Purchase forms the perfect silhouette of a twenty-two-year-old woman wearing a bikini."

"What's that?" Lenny Bell asked, pointing to the Mississippi River.

"One of her straps has come untied," Mr. Wilson said.

While I respected Mom's values, I had been toying with the notion that being alone might actually be better than dating scum.

"Mr. Wilson's dating the French teacher," I said.

"Hmmm," Mom said, biting her lip. "Frenchwomen are tough competition."

"And," I tattled, "he talks about IT all the time."

In Mom's world, there was nothing lower than a man who

talked about IT. According to Mom, if a man's doing it right, he doesn't have time to talk. Since Dad not only never discussed IT but left the room in a blue streak when the subject came up, Sis and I held him in the utmost esteem.

"Did you hear that?" Mom asked Dad, eyebrow arched. "Mr. Wilson talks about IT to his students!"

"She's making As, isn't she?" Dad mumbled as he fine-tuned the tinfoil on the TV rabbit ears.

"Mr. Wilson said the Louisiana Purchase looked like a girl in a bikini," I said, on a roll.

"Oh," Mom said, eyebrow coming in for a landing. "That's not bragging about IT. That's thinking about IT. There's a big difference. When a man stops thinking about IT, you might as well send him to the glue factory."

You won't find information like that in a textbook.

Fat Cat

I had a friend who tried to shoot a cat for walking on his brand-new Camaro. He blew out his windshield instead. When I asked him what he'd learned from this experience, he said, "Only shoot at fat cats."

"He isn't fat!" I say as I slop a can of tuna tidbits into Cat's bowl. "He's big-boned."

"There are belly prints on the car," Sweetie says, arms crossed.

"He has short legs!" I insist as I drop a handful of Tartar Control Tasty Treats on top of the tuna tidbits. "And his tiny head makes his body look bigger."

"If his gut drops any lower," Sweetie says, "he'll need platform pussy boots for his feet to touch the floor."

Huffing, I clang the side of the bowl with a spoon. Cracking one eye open, Cat yawns as he slowly pulls himself to a stand. At least I think he's standing. With the couch bowing, it's a little hard to tell. Rocking back and forth, he finally works up the momentum to roll off the couch. When he hits the floor, it sounds like someone dropped a bowling ball.

Waddling across the living room, Cat's stomach swings back and forth underneath him like those chamois strips at a car wash. If I sprayed a little Pledge on him, I'd never have to dust-mop again.

When Cat finally blubbers to a stop at my feet, it takes me a minute to figure out which end to put the bowl under. As much as I hate to admit it, when you can't find your pet's head, it's probably time to do a little soul-searching.

"All Cat needs is a little exercise," I say as I march Sweetie and Cat up the hill behind our house.

About a quarter of the way up, Sweetie and Cat leave me in their dust. When I finally manage to claw my way to the top, you can hear me gasping in New Jersey. I've sweated so much I'm dehydrated, and I'm pretty sure my lungs are about to explode.

Meanwhile, Sweetie, cigarette hanging on his lip, is doing chin-ups on a low-lying limb and Cat is leaping from log to log like a fat flying squirrel.

Since Cat obviously hasn't lost an ounce from our hike up the Catskills, I decide to go directly to Plan B.

"So," Dr. Dan says as his intern unlatches the door of Cat's carrying case, "we think Cat may be somewhat weight challenged?"

Pulling on his rubber gloves, Dr. Dan bends down and takes a peek inside.

"Good Gawd!" he gasps, jumping back. "What is that thing?!"

Taking a tentative peek inside the cat carrier, the intern jams her fist in her mouth.

"How on earth did you get him in there?" Dr. Dan asks, taking a closer look.

"We assembled it around him," Sweetie says as he listens to his own heart with Dr. Dan's stethoscope.

"You have to take a test to drive a car," the intern fumes indignantly. "Apparently, any moron can own a cat!"

Sweetie rolls his eyes. In his book, *only* a moron would own a cat.

Giving me the evil eye, the interns flips her head in the air and goes for supplies. I'm beginning to suspect this woman may not have the necessary bedside manner to serve catkind. It is, after all, the moron who's paying the bill.

When the intern comes back, she's carrying a tiny bag that would fit in my purse.

"Wow!" I say, catching a glimpse at the price tag on the special scientific protein blend for inactive cats.

Tell me why food with 25 percent less fat costs 50 percent more than the stuff that tastes 100 percent better.

While Dr. Dan explains the new diet to Sweetie, I try to comfort Cat.

"Don't worry," I whisper to the tufts of hairy blubber oozing out of the carrier, "I won't let them starve you."

Reaching inside, I scratch Cat under his fuzzy chin. At least I'm hoping it's his chin.

The Hangman

Mom, Sis, my niece, and I are on our annual pilgrimage to Dollywood Theme Park. If you've never been to a country music theme park, think Disney does *Deliverance*.

"Whelp," my niece, Cortney, says, checking off the Grizzly River Rampage and the Screaming Delta Demon on our park map, "that's every ride except . . . *The Hangman*."

Sis narrows her eyes at me. If looks could kill, I'd be sitting on cloud nine and discussing the decay of country music with Patsy Cline.

After years of anticipation, Cortney is finally tall enough to ride the ultimate in amusement park terror—The Hangman. And after pleading, pouting, and throwing tantrums, I've almost got Sis talked into letting me take her.

Cortney and I were cut from the same cloth. They haven't made a ride we won't barf for.

Mom and Sis, on the other hand, are wussies with a capital P. Mom gets motion sickness walking through the turnstile at the entrance, and you won't get Sis on the Carousel until they install air bags on the pink pony.

"Hangman . . . Hangman . . . Hangman . . ." Cortney and I chant as we drag Mom and Sis past the singing guitars.

Somewhere between the Space Dot Ice Cream and funnel cakes, we lose Mom. We finally find her at the petting zoo soaking her feet in the duck pond.

"I told you to wear comfortable shoes," I say.

"And I told you to major in medicine!" Mom snaps as she beats a duck away from her corn dog with her purse.

Before they haul Mom off for mauling mallards, we move on.

"Hangman . . . Hangman . . . Hangman . . ."

Rounding the corner, we stop dead in our tracks. Standing in the shadow of the King of Amusement Park Pain, we slowly look up. Standing on steel beam legs like a giant rusty dinosaur, the Hangman scrapes and groans.

"What kind of disturbed mind thinks these things up?" Mom mutters.

Sis lights a cigarette.

Traveling faster than the speed of sound, a blur of gaping mouths rips past us. This is followed by blood-curdling screams that only people having tonsils yanked out without anesthesia could produce. I'm thinking, one stripped screw, and they'd have to do a DNA test to identify the grease spot.

Clothes shredded and gripping the remains of their scalps, wild-eyed Hangman survivors straggle past us.

"Ready to spit up your guts?" the kid in line in front of us asks.

"Your last name wouldn't happen to be Kevorkian, would it?" I ask.

"Why do they make you take off your shoes?" Cortney whispers.

"So you won't get pee all over them," Kid Kevorkian says knowingly.

Very quietly, Cortney starts inching backwards.

"Hey, piece of cake!" I crow, totally confident that Billy Ray Cyrus will be singing Figaro at the Met before Sis lets Cortney get near this death trap.

Sis takes one last drag off her cigarette, then flicks it into her Slurpee cup.

"Cortney," Sis sighs, bending down, "for years, all you've talked about is riding The Hangman."

Glasses teetering on the tip of her nose, Cortney looks up into her mom's face.

"If you don't do this, sweetheart," Sis says quietly, "you'll regret it."

White-knuckled and heart in my throat, I stare down at my shoeless feet. I wonder if morticians do pedicures. I'd hate to spend eternity with unkempt cuticles.

"I just want you to know," Cortney says, taking her glasses off, folding them, and handing them to me for safekeeping in my fanny pack, "if anything happens to me, my mom is going to kill you."

Stretching, Kid Kevorkian leers back at us over his seat.

"You know the *really* great thing about The Hangman?" he says as the attendant welds the padded safety bar down on us. "When you throw up, it doesn't land on you."

Dust Bunnies and
the Mafia Maid

Basically, men and women are looking for the same qualities in a person—someone who's dependable and honest who'll scrub the toilet once a week.

"Did you make a list?" Maxine asks, calling from her car phone.

"A list?" I ask as I sling dirty dishes into the dishwasher.

"You have to spell out what you want," Max says, "or she'll run all over you."

"I need a prenuptial with my housekeeper?" I ask as I Windex every surface in the kitchen, including the cat.

"Trust me," Max says knowingly. "You're on your 'housekeeper honeymoon' right now. It'll pass."

I'm doing the fifty-yard dash with the dust mop when the housekeeper's '98 Lincoln rolls to a stop next to my '87 Honda in the driveway. Throwing the mop down the basement steps, I survey the house. It's never been cleaner.

The housekeeper is following me into the living room when Cat jogs past with a mouse dangling from his mouth. I should have the housekeeper sign a nondisclosure form along with her prenuptial.

"What I had in mind," I say as I nonchalantly grab the

mouse by its tail and toss it out the French doors, "would be like a deep spring cleaning . . ."

When I think clean, I think Grandma's house. Sunlight twinkling through an ammonia haze, bleach burning your nose, and the oven fuming in a caustic oven-cleaner meltdown. Avoiding sunlight like a vampire wasn't the only reason Grandma had beautiful skin. Cleaning day was equivalent to a fifteen-hundred-dollar chemical peel.

". . . wax the baseboards, vacuum under the furniture, wash the windows . . ."

"I don't do windows," the housekeeper interrupts. "I don't do ovens, garages, attics, or unfinished basements."

Add laundry to that list, and we could be twins separated at birth.

While the housekeeper bonds with my baseboards, I run to call Leila. "She's here," I whisper, hand cupped over the phone.

"Well," Leila says, "I hope she doesn't steal too much."

"*What?*" I say, taking the phone into the closet.

"She cleans me out every time," Leila says. "Remember my silver fox? I saw a woman wearing it yesterday."

"Who wears fur in summer?"

"Apparently, it's all the rage down at the meat packing plant."

"So you pawned her off on me?"

"Other than the sticky fingers," Leila says, "she's not that bad."

On that note, I crack the closet door to check on the housekeeper. She's munching on a Triscuit and thumbing through *Good Housekeeping.*

"Besides," Leila adds, "what do you have that's worth stealing?"

Be that as it may, for the next two hours I sit in the closet and work myself into a paranoid frenzy. For all I know, this woman could be the queen of an international ring of Mafia Maids. At exactly two o'clock there's a tap on the closet door, and I almost jump into the clothes hamper.

Snapping off her black rubber gloves, the housekeeper hands me her bill. This woman charges more per hour than my gynecologist. "You wanna check my work?" she asks.

Pushing the curtain of cobwebs aside, I walk into the dining room. You could write the Gettysburg Address in the dust on the shelves and plant corn in the crumbs under the table.

"Looks great!" I say, shoving a check into the housekeeper's hand and rushing her toward the door.

"Same time next week?" she asks, already penciling me into her Day-Timer.

I'm about to tell this woman that Hades will be a ski resort before she sets foot in my house again when it occurs to me—if I make the Mafia Maid mad, I might not have any windows to clean.

"Sure," I sigh.

Getting rid of a housekeeper is like getting a divorce. Sometimes it's cheaper to keep her.

Fruitcake

Anyone who doesn't like fruitcake has never tasted my great-aunt May's. She doesn't slice it; she pours it by the shot. Four bites and you're hung over until New Year's.

"Did you remember the *flavoring*?" Aunt May asks as she wipes her hands on her apron.

Setting the cardboard box on the table, I start unloading bottles. From what I can tell, the secret to good fruitcake is absorbency. Aunt May's fruitcakes soak it up like Pampers.

"Tupperware is the best thing since indoor plumbing," Aunt May says as she glugs half a bottle of flavoring over a cake. "Mother's fruitcake would eat right through a cake tin."

Back then, the family's flavoring came from a still in the holler behind the barn. It was strictly for medicinal purposes.

I'm on my way out the door with the empties when Aunt May's next-door neighbor suddenly storms past me. "Miss May!" Mr. Montgomery thunders. "I am not staring at that abomination again this year!"

Frowning, I glance out the kitchen window at Aunt May's life-size nativity scene. Propped between Joseph and the shepherds keeping watch stands jolly old Saint Nick. Raising the tacky factor of this setting, Aunt May has used my old Thumbelina doll for baby Jesus and draped gold chains and hoop earrings on the Wise Men.

With silver tinsel blowing, baby Jesus's arms and feet kicking, Santa clanging bells, Rudolph's red nose blinking on and off, and the Wise Men resembling three rap singers from the South Side, the front yard looks like Bourbon Street during Mardi Gras.

"It's festive!" Aunt May snaps, eyes narrowed and lips pursed.

"It's obscene!" Mr. Montgomery sputters, red-faced.

Standing face to face, they glare at each other, fists clenched. Then, suddenly, Aunt May breaks into a dazzling southern belle smile.

"Fruitcake, Mr. Montgomery?" she coos charmingly.

I come from women who firmly believe that there would be peace in the Middle East if they ate better baked goods.

Scooping up a glob of candied fruit goo, Aunt May slaps it on a plate and hands it to him.

"Certainly is moist," Mr. Montgomery observes, weighing the plate in his hand. "Has it been blessed?"

"By the Reverend Jack Daniels himself," Aunt May assures him, hands folded in front of her.

Judging by the puddle the cake is floating in, *baptized* would be more accurate.

Skeptically taking a bite, Mr. Montgomery proceeds to inhale the fruitcake, washing it down with a cup of Aunt May's eggnog—which is around 10 percent egg and 90 percent nog.

"Miss May, this isn't your fault," Mr. Montgomery says as he wipes his mouth with a Christmas napkin. "It's your woman's nature."

"My woman's nature," Aunt May echoes.

"Eve." Mr. Montgomery nods solemnly. "Without a husband, a woman naturally reverts to her heathen nature."

On that note, my old-maid aunt—whose famous caramel cakes built the west wing of the Cumberland Presbyterian Church—shoves another piece of fruitcake at him.

Mouth munching, Mr. Montgomery rolls an accusing eye at Aunt May like he suspects she's hiding the Tree of Knowledge behind the coffee percolator.

"This fruitcake certainly is . . . flavorful," Mr. Montgomery smacks.

Aunt May pours him another eggnog.

Mr. Montgomery is still lapping holiday cheer in a takeout cup when Aunt May shows him the door.

"Do come again," she sings, pushing him onto the porch.

Noses pressed to the window, Aunt May and I watch Mr. Montgomery weave and stagger across the lawn.

"That boy never could hold his fruitcake," Aunt May tuts.

When Mr. Montgomery gets to Aunt May's nativity, he stops. Wavering from side to side, he suddenly throws back his arm and catches Santa with a solid right hook.

Santa goes down for the count, then, after a few seconds, slowly begins to rise. Eyes wide and mouth gaping, Mr. Montgomery stares at Santa as if he's witnessing the resurrection.

"You anchored Santa with bungee cords," I say.

"The weatherman was calling for high winds," Aunt May says matter-of-factly.

Gaining momentum, Santa rebounds like Muhammad Ali, ramming Mr. Montgomery right in the nose. Stumbling backwards, Mr. Montgomery trips over the Chick-Fil-A cardboard cow Aunt May salvaged out of the Dumpster and lands at Mary's ruby-red toenails.

Baby Jesus kicks, Santa clangs his bell, Rudolph blinks, and Mr. Montgomery, a stunned look on his face, stares straight ahead like a statue.

"God works in mysterious ways," Aunt May sighs knowingly.

The Bus Driver

My mother was into diversity before the rest of the world had ever heard of it. She collected people like stamps—the more exotic the postmark, the better. If you ever saw a white middle-class Protestant at our house, he was asking for directions.

"Who's that in the dining room?" Dad asked, peeking around the corner.

"Hare Krishnas," I said, not looking up from *Star Trek*.

Sprawled all over the shag carpet were women with bells on their toes and bald guys in white robes. "*Om, Om,*" they said, setting up a vibration that made the crystal in the china cabinet rattle.

"Where do these people come from?" Dad muttered.

"The airport," I said as I practiced my Vulcan salute.

A dedicated Trekkie, I felt it perfectly natural that our house was a space station for extraterrestrials.

Dad, on the other hand, was of the school that foreigners belonged in their natural habitat, Dad's definition of foreign being anyone who was not a blood relative (and several who were, but for whatever reason had been disqualified).

The only time Dad made an exception to this rule was for a good-looking woman with an accent. But that's another story.

Occasionally, having a weirdo-magnet for a mom really came in handy.

Maddie (which Lee Whipperman's mom said was short for *rabid female dog*) was our school bus driver. Maddie reminded you of a pit bull with a Winston hanging out of its mouth, except she lacked the pit's winning personality.

While most of the other bus drivers were cheerful rosy-cheeked moms looking for part-time jobs, Maddie was a Teamster who, it was rumored, had left Chicago under questionable circumstances. We were the only bus in the school system where the kids had smoker's hack and thought Jimmy Hoffa was the father of our country.

"Hey! You with the Winnie the Pooh lunch pail!" Maddie would yell into her rearview mirror. "Sit your *butt* in that seat, or the fish will be spreading your guts on a cracker!"

Either Maddie liked you or she didn't. And if she didn't, no matter how fast or how far you ran, you'd never catch her bus again.

I made a serious effort to be as inconspicuous as an overweight ten-year-old with horn-rim glasses and a volume of *Bullfinch's Mythology* under her arm could be. But one day I caught Maddie glaring at me in the rearview, and I knew my time had come.

"You remind me of a scab I once knew," she said, making a sucking sound through the gap in her front teeth.

I'd never had a scab I was particularly fond of, so I figured this was not good.

"My bus driver's going to spread my guts on a cracker," I informed Mom.

Mom's solution was to send me out to the bus stop with a cup of coffee.

"You trying to bribe me, kid?" Maddie asked, sniffing the cup.

I wasn't sure what a bribe was, but apparently it was highly effective. Maddie let me on the bus.

After about a week of coffee service, Maddie showed up

at our house early one morning before her shift, parked the school bus in our driveway, and came inside for breakfast with Mom.

"Who's that in the dining room?" Dad asked, peeking around the corner.

"My bus driver," I said as I packed my Mr. Spock lunch box.

". . . Anyone ever gives you any trouble," Maddie said to Mom, grinding her cigarette out in the remains of her eggs, "you let me know."

"Where do these people come from?" Dad muttered.

From a union hall far, far away.

Wholey, Wholey, Wholey

Book tours are a lot like running for a political office. After all is said and done, you might as well close your eyes, pucker up, and kiss that baby.

"What kind of television show is it?" I ask, staring at my round-trip ticket to Washington, D.C.

"It's no big deal," my publicist says as she pushes me down the hall. "Just a little round-table discussion."

"Who else is going to be on the show?" I ask.

"No one you've ever heard of," she assures me, hammering the elevator button.

"What are we going to talk about?"

"Nothing important," she says, shoving me inside the elevator.

Hands crossed in front of her, my publicist smiles placidly.

"My behind's cooked, isn't it?" I ask.

"Like a Butterball," she says as the elevator doors close.

Truthfully, I'm not all that concerned about discussing politics. Based on what I've seen on television, all you really need is an opinion. Facts, figures, and a knowledge of history just seem to get in the way.

Still, faced with the prospect of going on national TV, I decide I better bone up a bit. "So, what's your take on the next presidential race?" I ask.

"Gore will go virtually unchallenged in the primary. Senator Fred Thompson, with his strong presence and experience in acting, will most certainly be a force to be reckoned with," Tefarria, my Ethiopian cabdriver, says.

Armed with this insider information, I'm pumped and ready to take on the town.

Cheryl, the producer for *Dennis Wholey's America*, meets me in the lobby, takes one look at me, and says, "I think we better get you to makeup."

Debbie, the makeup girl, takes one look at me and pulls out the paint rollers and putty knives.

"Have you ever considered cutting your hair," Debbie casually chats as she sprays the first coat of primer, ". . . and maybe trimming an inch or two off the nose?"

One final fry with the curling iron and Debbie steps back so I can check out my reflection. I look like Betty Boop. Taking me by the arm (since I'm having a little trouble holding my head up with five pounds of makeup on), she leads me to the guest lounge with careful instructions not to make any facial expressions until I dry.

And there, lounging around the lounge, are my fellow panel members: Pat Schroeder, for twenty-two years a U.S. representative from Colorado, Geraldine Ferraro, the first female U.S. vice presidential candidate, Ben Wattenberg, host of *Ben Wattenberg's Think Tank*, and E. J. Dionne, a political columnist.

I think I'm starting to get a feel for the show's format. It's like a highbrow *Politically Incorrect*—and I'm the incorrect.

As Cheryl goes around the room introducing us, I try to retain all the details, but either my short-term memory is failing or I'm getting high on the hair-spray fumes. I try not to inhale.

"Last, but certainly not least, we have Ron Canada," Cheryl says proudly. "Ron played *Othello* at the Kennedy Center."

Thank you, Lord, an actor. Everyone knows an actor needs a script like the Eveready Bunny needs batteries. At least I won't be the dumbest kid on the block.

"Prior to acting, Ron was a news anchor here in Washington," Cheryl explains. "I guess there isn't much you don't know about the Hill, is there, Ron?"

Somebody plant me in cement and drop me in the Potomac.

"How'd it go?" Sweetie asks when I call him from the Washington airport.

"I came across like a naive, uninformed idiot with a negative IQ," I groan.

"That's never bothered you before," Sweetie says.

Raising my fist in the air, I make this pledge, "As God is my witness, I will never, ever criticize anyone in politics again!"

Read my lips.

Old Lovers

Old lovers are like socks. They always show up full of static cling and missing their mate.

"What do you mean, one of Sweetie's old girlfriends is coming to visit?" Mom asks.

"She's passing through town and wants to say hi," I say, holding the phone receiver with my shoulder.

There's silence on Mom's end while she reflects on how best to advise me.

"Move," Mom says.

I don't know what it is about Sweetie, but once he's dated a woman, she will eventually try to fly his friendly skies again. And if any more of Sweetie's old girlfriends pass through, we're going to need an air traffic controller.

But still, you have to wonder about the women in your man's past. You have to wonder if what they *aren't* says something about what you *are*. But mostly you wonder if you're still hot enough to blow them off the map.

"I like having a man women want, even after the relationship is over," I say. "It keeps me on my toes."

"Honey, you barely reeled him in the first time," Mom says dryly. "And frankly, your hooks are starting to get a little rusty."

"Mo-ther," I huff, "today's women do not hunt and trap men like wild game."

"That's because today's women are at home watching *Ellen*," she says.

"If Sweetie liked her," I say, with total confidence, "I'm sure I'll like her." Sometimes I'm so cool, I give myself chill bumps.

"Have *you* been watching *Ellen?*" Mom asks.

About this time I hear a car pull in the driveway.

"Well?" Mom demands.

"She's driving a new Mercedes," I say, peeking through the miniblinds.

The car door opens and a pair of legs slide into view.

"Well?"

Rich, slim, sophisticated, brunette . . .

"Uh-oh," I mutter.

"I'm coming!" Mom cries. "Don't let her in until I get there!" Mom lives on the West Coast and refuses to fly. By the time she gets here, this woman will have Sweetie stuffed and mounted over her Sealy Posturepedic.

While Mom's lighting a candle for me down at the cathedral, I greet Sweetie's old girlfriend at the door. Strolling past me, she drops her silver fox in my arms like I'm the game warden.

"Scotch on the rocks with a touch of Drambuie," she says before I offer.

Which, coincidentally, happens to be Sweetie's drink of choice.

Staring at me, she stirs her drink with her finger, then slowly licks her diamonds dry. "You're not what I expected," she says.

Yeah, well, I'm not what I expected either. Such is life.

"You're so . . . "—searching for the adjective, she tilts her perfectly coifed head—"earthy."

Now and then, you meet a woman who's your instant soul mate. Then there are the women you'd like to chop into tiny pieces, mix with some Tender Vittles, and feed to the cat.

"Mom," I sigh as I watch Sweetie walk his old girlfriend to

her car, "how can a man be attracted to two women who are so different?"

"It's not how you bait the hook," Mom says. "It's how you dangle it in front of them."

At that moment Sweetie's old girlfriend appears to be dangling her tongue down Sweetie's throat like a night crawler.

"And a bottom dweller," Mom adds, "will jump at anything."

The Nurture of Your Bushiness

"Hold deet!" the guard barks, hand perched over his .45. "Stet your destiny and the nurture of your bush-iness!"

I'm standing in the lobby of my cousin's high-rise office building. As soon as I figure out what my destiny is, this guy will be the first to know. As far as the "nurture of my bushiness," I'm here to drink a little coffee and talk a little trash.

"Cooo-zens, eh?" the guard says skeptically. "Dere is no rez-ambulance."

"We had different parents," I say.

"Ahhh," the guard nods, "that ex-changes ev-reee-theeng."

Leading me to the elevator, he punches Joni's floor.

"You tell cooo-zen I say *buona sera!*" He winks as he combs his fingers through his hair.

"You got it." I wink back.

Just what my family needs, another failure to communicate.

The elevator rocks to a stop on my cousin's floor, and I saunter into her office.

"Hold, please . . . Hold, please . . . Hold, please . . ." the receptionist says into her headset.

"I'm here to see my cousin Joni," I explain between calls.

"You look so much alike," the receptionist bubbles, "you could be, like, related!"

The phone buzzes and the receptionist goes back to putting people on permanent hold. This is an insurance company, so it's not like anyone will notice.

"Kind of claustrophobic in here without a window, isn't it?" I chitchat.

Looking up from her switchboard, she glances around the room. "Wow," she says, wide-eyed, "there are no windows in here!"

"How long have you worked here?"

"Two years," she chirps.

I have no idea how long I've been waiting, but I'm pretty sure, any minute now, some guy in a three-piece suit is going to walk in, slap an anniversary pin on me, and tell me I'm vested.

I'm about to suggest we page Joni again when the receptionist suddenly bounces out of her chair.

"Time to shred!" she announces gleefully. Bouncing around the counter, she leans down into my face and whispers, "I'm in charge of shredding all the *confidential* documents."

"Is that confidential?" I whisper back.

Frowning, she gives this some thought. "I'll have to get back with you on that," she finally says.

"No hurry," I say.

"I really . . . *really* love to shred," she shivers. Then, with every line on the switchboard blinking and buzzing, the receptionist disappears around the corner, the cord of her headset swinging behind her.

I almost have my hand shadows perfected for the Itsy Bitsy Spider, when the receptionist suddenly sticks her head around the corner.

"You want to see my new shredder?" she asks. "It's the Model 2000."

Oh, why not.

"I burned the last one up," she says as we stare down at the shredder. "But this baby eats paper clips for breakfast."

She flips a toggle switch and it sounds like the space shuttle taking off. The room is vibrating so hard, my teeth are chattering.

"Don't stick your hand there," she yells in my ear, pointing to the row of razor blades slicing up and down.

Then she hands me a pile of reports and I slide them into the man-eating slot. "Ooooh," I squeal as hundreds of documents some manager no doubt spent weeks preparing are sliced into ribbons.

"Cool, huh?" she yells.

"Man, I love the nurture of your bush-iness!" I yell.

The Linguists

While I was born south of the Mason-Dixon Line, I grew up in Alaska. My grandmother, who considers Boston baked beans ethnic cooking, says I'm bilingual. My mouth swings either way.

Leila, Cuz, and I are sitting on the front porch of Russell's Store watching the rain fall. We're drinking bottled Cokes, the little ones, and Leila has poured a bag of peanuts into hers. Being half Yankee, I take my peanuts on the side.

"She's a good rain," an old man rocking at the other end of the porch says.

Leaning sideways, the man next to him spits tobacco into a coffee can on the floor. "Slow and steady," he says, wiping his mouth with the back of his hand, "like a good woman."

In our neck of the woods, "politically correct" means mounting your Rush Limbaugh sticker on the right side of the bumper.

It's the noise that gets our attention first. Actually, more of a vibration pounding over the sound of the rain that's tap-dancing on the tin roof.

"It's the Boss," Cuz says, identifying the beat as Bruce Springsteen.

Cuz is kind of an idiot savant when it comes to music. Being a certified psychologist, she's also kind of an idiot, but we love her.

Swiveling our heads, we watch headlights feel their way down the blacktop. There's a faded DUKAKIS FOR PRESIDENT sticker on the front bumper, so even before the car rolls to a stop, you know these people are lost.

Holding notebooks over their heads, two guys make a dash for the porch.

Suddenly Cuz drops her feet off the porch rail and sucks in her stomach, which is the universal sign for "Babe on Board."

As the guys walk past us, the three of us lean forward.

"Nothing I like more than a man whose good-bye is as good as his hello," Leila says as the screen door slams behind them.

By the time the guys return to the porch, the rain has reached critical mass and thunder is grumbling like Satan with a bad hand at a poker game.

"We're linguists," the first man says as he wipes the top of his Pepsi can with a paper napkin.

". . . traveling the back roads of the rural South on a federal grant . . ." his sidekick adds as he sniffs a vacuum-sealed hoagie.

". . . gathering data with the hopes of documenting the southern dialect," the first guy concludes.

"Well, shut my mouth," Leila drawls. "Who sez the federal deficit is the result of friv-vo-lous spendin'?"

"Shore wish you boooyz could be here at night," I say, licking each word like it's Neapolitan ice cream melting down a sugar cone on a hot summer day. "Them beetles bounce off that there screen like a pick on a steel git-tarrr."

Stretching like a cat, Cuz leans back in her rocker and throws one long tanned leg up on the porch rail. Being a psychologist, she recognizes the importance of body language.

The rest of the afternoon, we girls dedicate ourselves to science. When the professors' handheld tape recorders run out of tape, it's time for them to go.

"Y'all come back now, yuh hear?" we girls wave from the porch.

As the old man at the end of the porch watches the forest-green Volvo drive away, the man next to him leans sideways and spits into his coffee can.

"Don't believe there's a road goin' where them boys is tryin' to git."

The Realtor

"And this," the Realtor says as she sprays the doorknob with Lysol, "is a wonderful little fixer-upper."

Swinging open the door, my cousin and I drag ourselves into the foyer of yet another house. I promised Cuz I'd help her house-hunt, but I have to tell you, after two weeks of door to door I'm starting to feel like a Jehovah's Witness.

"Notice the lovely hardwood floors and the fireplace," the Realtor says, sweeping her hand through the air as she moves briskly through the room.

"Oooh," Cuz says, running her hand along the mantel.

"Lovely, isn't it?" the Realtor says brightly.

You know you've entered the later stages of house hunting when the Realtor describes a knothole as Picassoesque, and you nod in total agreement.

"Why is there a bed in the dining room?" I ask, peeking through the French doors.

"The previous owner must have forgotten it in the move," the Realtor chirps.

"It's nailed to the floor," I say, checking out the four-inch spikes at each bedpost. The only thing that's going to move this baby is an exorcism.

"Nothing a little wood putty won't fix," the Realtor assures my cousin.

We wander up the stairs and come to what most women consider the most important room of the house.

"Just look at the size of this bathroom!" the Realtor exclaims as she ushers us into the room.

"Wow!" Cuz says. "A whirlpool!"

"Big enough for three," the Realtor says.

"Exactly what did the previous owner do for a living?" I ask as Cuz climbs into the tub, leans back her head and simulates a hot soak after a hard day.

"I believe," the Realtor says, tilting her perky face sideways and tapping her Colorstay lipstick with a perfectly manicured nail, "she ran a little cottage industry out of the home. Why do you ask?"

"Oh," I shrug, "it's just not that often you see a master bath equipped with a for-pay wet bar and a condom dispenser."

"Moving on," the Realtor sings as she waves over her shoulder.

Cuz and I cling to each other as we feel our way down the dimly lit hall. "Maybe if they'd used brighter bulbs," Cuz whispers, "they wouldn't have needed to number the doors."

"What's in this room?" I ask, stopping at door number 3, which the Realtor obviously overlooked on her way down the hall.

Swinging the door open, Cuz and I come to a dead stop.

"The previous owner collected antique wrought iron," the Realtor says as Cuz slips both wrists into a lovely example of antique iron workmanship dangling on the wall. Spanish Inquisition period would be my guess.

". . . and leather," the Realtor adds as I hold up a black-leather mask with matching elbow-length gloves and knee-high boots.

"Aren't torture chambers normally located in the cellar?" Cuz asks, turning the wheel on the rack.

"Maybe this is the guest torture chamber," I say.

"Shall we take a look at the rest of the house?" the Realtor urges as Cuz and I snoop through the easy drip candles, feathers, and a simply lovely pair of fake diamond-studded handcuffs.

"I don't think that will be necessary," I say, heading for the door.

"Well," the Realtor says, handing me a slip of paper, "this is the asking price."

"You will change the blinking red light on the front porch," I say, re-counting the zeros to make sure I didn't miss one.

"Consider it done," the Realtor says, making a note on her clipboard.

"And," Cuz adds, "stipulate in the contract all possessions go with the house."

The Realtor and I turn to look at her.

"Hey," she says, cracking a whip, "I'm a single parent with two teenagers!"

The Birdhouse

Sweetie calls bird feeders bird welfare. He says it's just a matter of time before perfectly healthy birds lose their work initiative and quit doing whatever it is that birds do.

Sweetie and I are at the Lawn and Garden Show, where every year hoards of crazed gardeners fervently vow to roll in manure, bathe in Miracle-Gro, and pledge allegiance to the *Farmer's Almanac*.

As far as I'm concerned, it's the best show on earth. Where else can you attend a four-hour lecture on how to design an award-winning flower arrangement out of a head of cauliflower?

While Sweetie is kicking tractor tires and talking lawn mowers with the other good ol' boys, I head for the yard accessories.

My mission, as it has been for the past three years, is to find the perfect birdhouse—a birdhouse that I would live in if I were a bird. According to Sweetie, I have the featherbrain, all I'm missing is the appetite.

The first booth I come to looks like a cost-cutter trailer park. The birdhouses have been stamped out of recycled tomato cans and spray-painted by a robot. The salesman presses a button and the top pops off like a jack-in-the-box. "For quick cleaning," he says, turning it upside down and thumping the rusty bottom.

Frankly, I'd rather not attract birds that would settle for a third-rate romance, low-rent rendezvous in a rusty double-wide with Arkansas plates.

In the next booth, the salesman is pushing hillbilly outhouses. "It can be used as a birdhouse . . . or a toilet paper holder," the salesman says as he slides a roll of Charmin onto the perch.

I move on before he decides to pull any other toilet features out of his birdhouse.

"A Rubbermaid birdhouse?" I ask at the next booth.

The salesman slams the birdhouse on the floor and it bounces back into his hand.

"You've never actually seen a bird, have you?" I ask the salesman.

This flies over his head like a martin.

The antebellum birdhouse has stuffed cardinals dressed as the cast from *Gone With the Wind*. You can tell a lot about a man by the birdhouse he builds. This cuckoo belongs in the Rubbermaid.

After breathing fermenting mulch all day, I can barely walk a straight line. So, at first I think it's a mirage. There is only one birdhouse left in the booth—and it's perfect.

Wild grapevines twist around knotty cedar and green moss spreads across the bark walls like it grew there. It's all I can do to keep from plopping my fluffy white tail down and laying an egg.

I'm pulling out the checkbook when I notice a woman coming in for a landing on my right. She's cooing at my birdhouse like a homing pigeon.

"Finders keepers!" I declare, grabbing the birdhouse.

"I'll pay you twice your asking price!" the woman says to the salesman.

"Sorry," the salesman says, prying our hands off the birdhouse. "It's not for sale."

"What do you mean, it's not for sale?!" we crow in unison.

"It's a display," he says.

"All right, all right!" the woman snaps. "Just tell me the company that manufactured it, and I'll order one over the Internet."

"It wasn't manufactured," the salesman says. "It's a real nest."

"*Real?*" the woman cringes as she immediately starts checking herself for lice.

"Wow," I say, taking a closer look. "You mean a bird actually built it?"

"Believe it or not," the salesman says dryly, "there are still a few birds out there not living in public housing."

The Haircut

"I can make you look ten years younger," he whispers in my ear.

According to my hairdresser, I am now too old to wear my hair long. Where has the time gone? It seems like only yesterday when Mom taped a bow on my bald head so people wouldn't think she was breast-feeding a bowling ball.

Cheek to cheek, Sergie and I stare at my reflection in the mirror. As far as I'm concerned, the hair is the least of my problems. There was a time when I didn't go to bed looking this bad.

"I can't cut my hair, Serge," I say. "It's my only good asset."

"Then consider yourself bankrupt," he says dryly.

I'm a low-maintenance kinda girl. Basically, my hair-care routine consists of wadding the whole mess into a bun. If anything sticks out, I whack it off. Needless to say, Sweetie is very careful about keeping his assets safely stowed.

"A little snip here, a little snip there," Sergie tempts as he clicks his scissors in the air like castanets. "You won't feel a thing."

"Will I still feel sexy with short hair?" I ask, biting my lip.

"Oh, please," Sergie says, rolling his eyes. "Remember Sharon Stone? For years, a long-haired nobody. Then she cut her hair into a sassy little cut and voilà—*Basic Instinct.*"

Sweetie saw *Basic Instinct* six times. Not once did he walk out of the theater talking about the hair on Sharon Stone's head.

"Sweetie doesn't like short hair," I say, chewing on a nail. "He says he doesn't date G.I. Joes."

"Well," Serge sniffs, "to each his own."

Who's a girl to trust? Her fashion-savvy hairdresser or her Sweetie—the man who finds it perfectly acceptable to wear black dress socks with white tennis shorts?

"It was hard for my ex-wife to cut her hair, too," Sergie says as he swings a lilac apron around my neck.

"You were married—to a woman?" I ask in disbelief.

"That girl never had it so good," Sergie sighs as he tucks a towel around my neck. "I cooked. I cleaned. I waxed her mustache."

Tilting my chin up, Sergie checks my upper lip for peach fuzz. It's just a matter of time before I'll be coming in for a shave and a haircut.

"Why didn't it work out?" I ask. "Was it because you're . . . a hairdresser?"

"I'd say that was probably the straw that broke the camel's back," he says.

Sergie plucks the bobby pins out of my bun and my limp hair drops like a rag. Sucking in a breath, he throws his fist to his mouth and bites his knuckle.

"Ssss-sweet Bette Davis!" he gasps. Narrowing his eyes, Sergie bends down to get a closer look. "What is this?!" he demands, picking up a multi-bleached strand, the result of a botched home highlight.

"I tried to touch up the roots," I confess sheepishly.

"Why don't you just buy a Do-It-Yourself Surgery Kit at Super-X and give yourself a nose job?!" he snaps.

Do they sell those?

Before I know what's happening, Sergie grabs his scissors

in one hand and a wad of my hair in the other. "You'll thank me when this is over," he says, cramming my hair in the scissors.

Holding my breath, I stare at my face in the mirror. With one snip I will be transformed into a stylish, sophisticated conservative lady . . . absolutely none of the qualities Sweetie looks for in a woman.

"Wait!" I scream.

"Aaaggghhh!" Sergie screams back, grabbing his heart.

"I can't do it!" I cry. "I just am what I am!"

"Ohhhh!" Sergie says, dropping his wrist. "That's exactly what I told my ex-wife!"

An Honorable Coon Dog

"What a waste of time!" Sweetie says as he shoves a tree limb out of the way. "A good coonhound would never hurt a cat."

"Sweetie," I say, slapping a mosquito, "you wouldn't know a coon dog from a corn dog."

It's the middle of the night and Sweetie and I are clawing our way through briers and brambles in search of my cat, Cat. Meanwhile, off in the distance coon dogs are running through the foggy woods of our farm, howling like the Hounds of the Baskervilles.

"Exactly how does one distinguish a good coon dog from one that's gone bad?" I huff and puff as I crawl after Sweetie up the hill. "Do they howl with a private school accent?"

"Cat can take care of himself," Sweetie calls back over his shoulder. "He'll climb a tree."

"Oh, please!" I wheeze. "If he gains another ounce, we'll have to hoist him into his litter box with a crane!"

I am not opposed to hunting. I just have a small problem with armed drunken rednecks chasing the hounds of hell through my backyard between the hours of midnight and three.

Furthermore, Cat doesn't resemble any animal known to man. He doesn't have a tail and he's built like Son of Flubber. If I saw the furry glob oozing toward me on a tree limb, *I'd* shoot him.

We finally make it to the top of the hill. While I'm bent over double, gripping my side and spitting blood, Sweetie has his head cocked like a beagle and is listening to the wind.

"You go that way," he says, pointing into total darkness.

I'm about to tell Sweetie where he can go when a blood-curdling howl pierces the air. Without a thought, I take off into the abyss.

As I hack my way through blackberries with my flashlight and splash through the freezing creek, my imagination runs wild.

I see poor Cat trembling on a limb. Below him, cat-killing coon dogs, foaming at the mouth and hopped up on Junkyard Dog Chow, snap and rip at the tree. Meanwhile, inbred Neanderthals, their drunken laughter echoing through the holler, pass the jug.

"What d'yu reckon that thang is, Bob Bart Billy Boy?" Bubbah asks, scratching his gut through his overalls.

"Looks tuh me like a giant tick with fur uh-polstry," Bob Bart Billy Boy says as he squirts tobacco juice between the gap in his teeth.

"Hey-elll, let's shoot the dang thang and feed it tuh the dawgs!"

Fists clenched and adrenaline pumping, I storm into the clearing, fully prepared to fight off rabid coon dogs, armed with nothing but spunk and a felt-tip highlighter pen.

"Hey, you!" I holler through clenched teeth.

The Coon Man spins around, and one can't help but notice, he's wearing the ever-stylish J. Paul Peterman all-weather safari jacket.

"You're trespassing!" I yell, slightly deterred by the fashion statement but still breathing hard. "Get that vicious pack of kitty-killing coon dogs off my property!"

My message doesn't carry quite the punch I'd hoped for, what with a floppy-eared coon dog with soulful brown eyes licking my hand.

"Madame," the hunter says, using the classic Oxford pronunciation, "a good coon dog would never hurt a cat."

Do men have a monthly newsletter that updates them on junk like this?

When I return to the house, I'm dripping wet, draped in poison ivy, and probably have tetanus from my run-in with a rusty barbed-wire fence. Meanwhile, Sweetie and Cat—not a cat hair out of place—are stretched out on the couch watching *Baywatch*.

"Man," Sweetie says, tossing a handful of popcorn in the vicinity of his mouth, "you look rough."

As much as I would simply love to sit and chat, there's an unidentified varmint crawling up my leg, and I suspect his intentions are less honorable than a good coon dog's.

General Lee

"Do you run out of gas often, dear?" Mrs. Montgomery asks as she refills my cup.

"Not as often as I used to," I say, helping myself to another tea cake.

"With age comes responsibility," Mrs. Montgomery nods knowingly.

Actually, with New Age cars comes a little gas-pump icon that glows on the dashboard. If they ever come out with a car that sends an electric shock through the steering wheel, I'll never run out of gas again.

"Have you considered keeping the tank full?" Mrs. Montgomery asks, head tilted attentively.

"I tend to live on the edge," I say. Or on the shoulder, depending on one's perspective.

Shortly after I decided to take the scenic route home, my car coasted to a stop in front of Mrs. Montgomery's antebellum mansion. You'd have thought she was expecting me.

"We don't get many visitors anymore, do we, General Lee?" Mrs. Montgomery says, patting the mop of moth-eaten fur standing beside her chair.

General Lee hasn't taken his beady black eyes off of me since I straggled to the door. According to Mrs. Montgomery, General Lee is a pedigreed Pomeranian. He looks more like a piranha with fur to me. He has pointed little rat teeth, and despite the painted toenails and bows in his hair, smells like something the cat dragged in.

"Don't your kids come to visit you?" I ask, taking a sip of tea.

"Unfortunately," Mrs. Montgomery sighs, "none of my husbands could have children."

"Husbands?"

"Seven," Mrs. Montgomery says, holding up seven diamond-covered fingers. "I've outlived seven husbands and six Pomeranians, haven't I, General Lee?"

"Wow," I say. "I couldn't name seven guys I'd share a Coke with."

"Well, dear," Mrs. Montgomery says, leaning over the cookie tray with her finger to her chin, "men are a lot like gasoline. I've tried high test and I've tried regular, and there isn't a dime's difference between the two."

Gingerly selecting a cookie off the tray, Mrs. Montgomery crams it into the Pomeranian's mouth. "Tea cake, General Lee?"

Glaring at me, General Lee doesn't even bother to lick the crumbs off.

"All my husbands came to live with me here," Mrs. Montgomery says, waving the cookie in the air. "I have their portraits hanging on my bedroom wall."

"You slept with seven husbands in the same bed, surrounded by portraits of your late husbands?" I say incredulously.

No wonder Mrs. Montgomery doesn't have kids. It takes the wind out of Sweetie's sail if he thinks the cat's watching.

Since our relationship has progressed to the girl-talk level, I feel it's safe to mention the smell.

"Mrs. Montgomery," I say, leaning toward her, "what's that smell?"

Mrs. Montgomery lifts her nose even higher and sniffs. "It's the smell of old money, dear," Mrs. Montgomery says, taking a genteel nibble off General Lee's hairy cookie. "People with old money have a very distinctive odor . . . much like people with cats."

On that note, I bury my nose in my T-shirt. If there is an underlying smell of cat, I'm pretty sure it's masked by Sweetie's cigarette smoke and a hint of Taco Bell.

"My third husband always said he could smell his sweat on his money," Mrs. Montgomery reminisces.

My guess is, it was his spit from counting the interest.

"Actually," I say, noticing there are buzzards circling outside the window, "this odor has more of a road-kill quality to it."

Giving this some thought, Mrs. Montgomery looks down at General Lee. Poking him with her finger, General Lee topples over on his side, his four little stiff paws sticking straight out.

"Apparently," Mrs. Montgomery sighs, "I'm not as stinking rich as I thought I was."

Chivalry

"Your generation is going to Hades in a convertible!" my great-aunt May declares.

"You're just jealous because yours had to walk," I say as I plunk her into a chair.

Every week, all of my great-aunts meet for the all-you-can-eat catfish at the City Café. By the end of the meal, I envy the catfish.

"In my day, a gentleman didn't talk about what went on behind the tobacco barn!" Aunt May snaps. "It was called chivalry!"

Nowadays, it's called perjury. But with cigar sales up 150 percent, I think we can safely assume the tobacco barn is still hopping.

"I'll have the fried catfish, fried corn, fried okra, and fried tomatoes," my great-aunt Dee rasps, holding the menu at arm's length and squinting. "And a fried apple pie for dessert."

"Hush puppies?" Loretta asks without looking up from her pad.

"Baked cornbread," Aunt Dee grumbles, tucking the menu back behind the napkin holder. "Dr. Jack says I need to start watching my cholesterol."

Dr. Jack also told Aunt Dee cigarettes were going to kill

her. So, after smoking two packs a day for fifty years, she switched to Marlboro Lights and breaks the filters off.

"Once, Mr. James Booth bragged that he'd kissed me," Aunt May says as she dumps four packs of sugar into her sweetened tea. "Your great-uncles took that boy out behind the barn and taught him some manners."

"So did you kiss him?" I ask, fishing a fried pickle out of a pool of Wesson oil.

"Maybe I did and maybe I didn't," Aunt May says, shrugging the Fifth. "In my day, a nice girl didn't talk about it."

"Well, I kissed him," Aunt Dee croaks. "It was like kissing that catfish."

Aunt May and I follow the bobbing tip of Dee's cigarette to the glassy-eyed catfish mounted on the wall. Aunt May catches the resemblance right off.

"Mr. Booth had a waxed handlebar mustache," she nods knowingly.

"And he was a little on the scaly side," Aunt Dee says, lips pursed in thought like a drawstring bag.

"Psoriasis," Aunt May explains.

"And, for as long as I live," Aunt Dee rasps, "I will never forget those cold, slimy lips."

They both give a little simultaneous shiver.

"Why on earth did you go out with him?" I ask, wiping my hands. For some reason, I've suddenly lost my desire for limp, greasy pickles.

"He was considered quite a catch in our day," Aunt Dee says, squinting as she puffs on her Marlboro.

"He had a car," Aunt May says, taking a sip of tea, puckering, then dumping two more packs in.

"A 1941 Ford Super Deluxe V-8 convertible," Aunt Dee rattles off. "Green as a ten-dollar bill."

"That car could fly," Aunt May smiles nostalgically as she stirs her tea slurry.

"So, one might say that women in your day were seduced by power," I say.

"No," Aunt Dee says, shaking her head. "I'd say it was money."

"Old money," Aunt May nods. "Those Booths owned the dinosaurs before they turned into oil."

"So, whatever happened to Mr. Booth?" I ask, greasy chin resting on my hand.

"He married a girl from up north," Aunt May says.

"Nashville," Aunt Dee nods.

"Of course," Aunt May sniffs, "marriage didn't slow him down any."

"If you want a man who never leaves the roost," Aunt Dee rasps as she stubs out her Marlboro in the Wesson oil, "don't marry a woodpecker."

The Change

Judging by my friends' mothers, women go through four developmental stages: (1) Gotta get a man. (2) Gotta get a house. (3) Gotta get a kid. (4) Gotta get a life.

Stage four is commonly referred to as the change of life, or by the more clinical term *men-on-pause*.

"I'm torn," Rosie's mother says, biting her lip. "If you were me, would you kayak across the Arctic Sea . . . or ride a camel across the Sahara?"

This strikes me as fairly adventurous for a woman who once told me God was going to burn me to a crisp for calling a boy on the telephone.

Flipping through the pile of travel brochures scattered on the table, I pick up a flier on white-water rafting in the Grand Canyon.

"I take it you're planning a little trip," I say.

"No," she says firmly. "I'm taking a BIG trip."

The tighter the coil, the farther it springs.

When Rosie and I were growing up, Mrs. Henry was the quintessential mom. There were always cookies in the cookie jar, and you could eat off her kitchen floor. While all the other sixties moms were burning their bras, Mrs. Henry held firmly to the notion that a woman without hair spray should have her children taken away.

Mrs. Henry always thought I was a bad influence on Rosie. The way she saw it, I was a wild girl who was destined for no good. In return, I called her Miz Er-ree. On top of my destiny of doom, she thought I had a speech impediment.

Gingerly sticking his head through the door, Rosie's dad clears his throat. "Dear," he says cautiously, "will we be having dinner tonight?"

Eyes narrowed and shoulders hunched, Mrs. Henry growls. Slowly, she turns to face him and, eyes wide as saucers, Mr. Henry runs for his life.

This strikes me as a tad bit cruel. After a lifetime in captivity, you can't just open the cage and tell a husband to go fend for himself. It's like tossing a goldfish on the pavement and saying, "Go find your own water."

Mrs. Henry cooked three meals a day—except on Sundays and her anniversary, when Mr. Henry treated her to Morrison's Cafeteria—every year of her marriage.

"That's 41,680 meals," she grumbles as she rips the tags off her new knapsack with her teeth, "not including cupcakes for all those blasted school parties."

Rosie is stunned. She just assumed being homeroom mother was the highlight of her mother's life.

Then one morning, Mrs. Henry looked in the mirror, and instead of seeing the Goddess of Blissful Domesticity, she saw a woman whose life was half over, and the only thing to show for it was fifty cookbooks.

"And it's all HIS fault!" she yells toward the den.

Suddenly, all the qualities that made Mr. Henry desirable in the first place—the stability, the security, the personality of a throw pillow—became the very things that seemed to be suffocating her.

Totally confused by the stranger in his bed, Mr. Henry didn't know whether to call a caterer or an exorcist.

Through the kitchen window, Rosie and I watch Mr.

Henry jog across the lawn to the divorcée's house next door. The "poisoned widow," as Mrs. Henry refers to her, has her door open and is fanning her scent throughout the neighborhood— pot roast.

"Will you be gone long?" Rosie frets, forehead wrinkled.

Mrs. Henry doesn't answer. And I suspect it's because the woman she used to be is never coming back.

"Take a long, hard look," Mrs. Henry warns ominously. "This is YOU in twenty years."

Rosie and I shudder.

"Well, not you," Mrs. Henry says, flippantly waving in my direction. "You've been wild as a snake all your life."

Under the circumstances, I take that as a compliment.

Hip Huggers

"Not every woman can wear this," the salesgirl says as she slips the dress out of my hands and hangs it back on the rack.

If this chick ate a grape, she'd look like a pregnant thermometer. I figure I can take her.

"Look," I say, lifting the dress back off the rack, "this ain't *Pretty Woman* and I'm not Julia Roberts."

"Too bad," the salesgirl says as she jerks the dress out of my hand and welds it back on the rack. "Because Julia Roberts is a size 4, and so is this dress."

I can't tell you what a thrill it is to discover that I was exactly the same size as Julia Roberts—during my first week of fetal formation.

"The main problem is your hips," the salesgirl notes as she scans me up and down using a wide-angle lens. "The rest of you seems fairly normal."

According to *Cosmopolitan*, the scientific journal for women with shoulder pads for brains, I am a "pear." In layman's terms, this means I'm shaped like a wide-body travel mug.

If you go by today's fashions, women with hips are an endangered species. Someday schoolchildren will gather around my skeleton while a teacher describes that time in history when women with giant hips walked the earth.

"Maybe we could camouflage them somehow," the salesgirl says, tapping her pouty lips with her finger.

Flipping through a rack of comfort-wear, she pulls out a pair of trousers and holds them up to me. The waist is exactly the same diameter as the hips.

"Excuse me," I say. "Do I look like a boa constrictor to you?"

I have an hourglass figure. My waist is fifteen inches smaller than my hips, and my breasts are . . . Okay, so I have a three-minute egg-timer figure.

My point is, if I buy pants that fit my hips, you could park a Volkswagen in the waistband. If I buy pants that fit my waist, I have to buy two pairs—one for each thigh.

"Look," I sigh, "surely there is something in this store I can wear."

Coming together in a Halston huddle, all the salesgirls stare at my hips like doctors conferring on how best to separate Siamese twins. "Not a thing," they finally say in unison.

"You're telling me that I'm the only woman left in this world with hips?" I demand.

"You know, they have surgery that can fix that now," the woman at the rack next to me says knowingly.

So this is what it's come to. I'm supposed to have the meat sucked off my bones in order to attract men who are attracted to women who look like boys.

"Gimme that dress!" I growl through gritted teeth.

Grabbing the hanger off the rack, I make a dash toward the dressing room. Weaving and ducking, I knock emaciated shoppers out of the way like *Night of the Living Dead*.

Finding an open stall, I run inside, slam the door, and slide the latch. On the wall is a little sign that reads: YOU STRETCH IT, YOU BUY IT.

Kicking off my Reeboks, I drop my jeans to the floor and toss my T-shirt on the hook. Stepping into the dress, I wiggle it into position, suck my belly button to my backbone, and zip. Holding my breath, I take a long, hard look at myself in the mirror.

I'd say it was a perfect fit—if I were an Oscar Meyer wiener. Not only can you see my panty lines, you can identify most of my major organs.

Of course, none of this matters anyway. I just caught a glimpse of the price tag. I can't afford the hanger, much less the dress.

The Past Has Passed

"And that was the year I wanted to open a Mexican restaurant," Mom says. "But your father wouldn't even consider it."

"Could it be because we're not Mexican?" I ask.

Mom isn't content with taking trips down Memory Lane. She's bought a condo and spends half the year there.

Having heard the Mexican restaurant story one billion times, I sort of drift off—which is unfortunate, since I'm driving.

"Aaaagh!" Mom screams.

I wake up just in time to see a garbage truck, with two burly guys hanging off the back, burning rubber down the part in my hair.

Spinning the steering wheel like the Wheel of Fortune, I grit my teeth and floor it. Our pickup truck bounces up onto the sidewalk, mows down a couple of hedges, then conveniently bumps back onto the pavement at a crosswalk.

Safely back on the road, I glance over at Mom. She's clinging to the roof like an albino bat.

"Stop the truck," she whimpers weakly. As soon as the truck rolls to a stop, Mom falls out face-first. Bent double, she pounds her chest and makes a strange little gurgling noise. She sounds just like the pump on my aquarium trying to prime itself after the electricity has gone off.

Swaying to a stand, Mom starts staggering down the sidewalk.

"You're going the wrong way," I call to her.

Jaw set, Mom keeps walking. Shifting the truck into first, I roll along beside her. I figure, in those shoes, how far can she get?

"How are we doing today?" a man calls from his front-porch rocker.

"My daughter tried to kill me," my mother calls back, with a little wave.

Amnesty International should list all daughters as prisoners of war.

"That was Wylie Wilson," Mom chats as she marches beside the truck. "You remember Wylie."

I stare at her blankly.

"When you were six years old, he bought you ice cream at the A&W drive-in." Mom stops to smell Mr. Wilson's roses. "A vanilla cone with a chocolate dip."

I am the only member in my family who wasn't blessed with a memory like flypaper. Mom considers it a birth defect.

"Hold the moment in an open hand," I say, "for the past has passed, and the future is but a dream."

Mom's face softens. "What is that from?" she asks, her head tilted in thought.

"I just made it up," I say.

"Oh, brother," Mom huffs, rolling her eyes.

Mom recognizes only two sources of wisdom—the Bible and Hallmark.

"You have no respect for your past," Mom tuts as she strolls down the sidewalk like she's on a tour of Williamsburg.

I'm a now kinda girl. As far as I'm concerned, the past is never real. People either glorify it or horrify it—or at the very least, colorize it.

"Mother," I sermonize, "if you spend your life thinking

about the past, you're going to miss the present. Then when the future gets here, you won't have anything to talk about."

Mom slows to a stop. Giving this some thought, she finally turns to face me. "You dropped out of the womb a little smart aleck," she says matter-of-factly.

Taking a deep breath, Mom resumes walking. "Which reminds me, sweetheart, of the time your grandmother gave you a Toni home perm. You looked just like Shirley Temple's evil twin."

Lift and Separate

"I've lost my bra," I say, head down in my suitcase and slinging clothes.

"What do you mean, you *lost* it?" Sweetie asks.

Under normal circumstances, it would take a lot more than lost undergarments to rattle me. But in one hour I'm giving a talk to a room full of people, and I'd just as soon the only thing quivering was my voice.

Lifting up the corner of the bedspread, Sweetie cautiously peeks under the bed as if the bra might slither out, rear up on its wire support, and hiss.

"Wear another one," he says, dropping the spread.

"I didn't bring another one," I say, turning my suitcase over and shaking it out onto the bed.

"You didn't bring a spare?"

"Don't go there," I warn as I cram my hand up a tennis shoe.

When it comes to packing, Sweetie and I are of two schools. I am a minimalist packer. I figure, unless I'm going to the moon, there will be stores.

Sweetie, on the other hand, packs like Noah—two of everything. This man lugged Campbell's soup, saltine crackers, and Vienna sausages with him to Europe—like we were going to get there and they wouldn't have food.

"How about using a Band-Aid?" Sweetie suggests, pulling out his OSHA first-aid kit. He holds up a Band-Aid that wouldn't cover a chigger bite.

"That's what you think of me?" I ask.

"Let's not go there," he mutters, sliding the first-aid kit back into his trunk.

Now, at this point a lot of men would throw up their hands and turn on the tube. Not my Sweetie.

"Okay," he says, lighting a cigarette. "Let's review. I take it going braless is not an option."

I hold up the blouse that I'm going to wear. It isn't Saran Wrap, but it isn't made of lead, either.

"It's Sunday. I don't suppose they sell ladies' under-garments at 7-Eleven?"

Suddenly a vision pops into my head of standing in front of a room full of people with two plastic Slurpee cups suc-tioned onto my boobs. Smalls.

"That means our only option, short of breaking into a lingerie shop, is to find the original piece of apparel," says Sherlock Sweetie. "When was the last time you saw it?"

I burst into the bicycle shop like I'm with the bomb squad. It's twenty minutes until show time. Sweetie's out in the car with the motor running, and the clock is ticking.

The place is packed with bicycle types, lean, bronzed, half-dressed guys in skin-tight bicycle pants—which when I become queen will be the mandatory uniform.

I finally spot a lone girl behind the cash register and make a dash toward her. "Yesterday we rented a couple of bikes and I changed in your dressing room," I whisper, stretching over the counter. "Did you happen to find a bra?"

"A bra?" the girl says, staring blankly at me. "I don't think so."

I think we can safely assume that the *I'm Fast* scrawled across her T-shirt does not refer to mental swiftness.

"HEY, SPEEDO!" she suddenly screams. "YOU FIND A
BRA IN THE DRESSING ROOM?"

Slowly I turn around to twenty biker eyes that are fixed on
me like a pack of coyotes.

"Looking for this?" Speedo asks, dangling my limp little
bra from his finger. One can't help but notice, there's a bicycle
tire track running diagonally across it.

"Thanks," I mutter, reaching for it.

Before I can take possession, Speedo jerks the bra back
and buries his face in it. "Hmmm," he sniffs. You've got to love
a man who finds Downy fabric softener erotic.

Meanwhile, one of the bikers continues to stare a hole
through me.

"I leave my underwear wherever I go," I say dryly as I stuff
the bra in my purse.

"Yeah?" the guy asks. "Where you headed next?"

Acknowledgments

Maureen O'Neal, Nancy Coffey, Dennie Burke, and Bill Carpenter—thanks isn't enough.